the beginner

VOLUME IX

flexographer

ARTWORK • ANILOX ROLLS • PLATES • PRESS • INKS • OPERATIONS • SUBSTRATES

FOUNDATION OF ftα

A compilation of the technical series originally published 2002 thru 2003 in FLEXO Magazine

Table of Contents

5. SUBSTRATES

6. PRODUCTIVITY & QUALITY CONTROL

The Beginner Flexographer Volume IX (TX-016) is published to disseminate information on topics of interest to flexographers. The viewpoints and conclusions expressed are those of the individual authors and not necessarily those of FTA/FFTA or FLEXO® Magazine. FTA/FFTA/FLEXO® imply no endorsement of such conclusions by publication of these reports.

Authors biographies appear as current on date of original publication.

CORRUGATED POSTPRINT

LIGHT-YEARS OF INNOVATION IN THE PAST DECADE

By Cordes Porcher

Over the past 10 years, the sheet-fed postprint corrugated flexo press has changed dramatically. Along with mechanical changes, expectations of the level of quality in this area of printing have also changed. The corrugated press—originally designed to "rotary rubber-stamp" black ink on a brown box—has metamorphosed into a piece of equipment capable of competing with offset labels, laminating and preprint liner.

These changes have not occurred at any one particular time, but have been a cumulative process, leading the way to improved operation, higher productivity, superior graphics and better working conditions for production staff.

Vacuum Transfer and Feeders

The first element to improve production and quality is the use of vacuum transfer. This conveyance system has allowed better sheet control, which allowed the postprint industry to improve its registration dramatically.

Recent modifications to this conveyance system allow zoning of the vacuum and controlling the amount of suction. These two improvements accommodate changes in sheet size, varying sheet thicknesses and varying liner porosities. Modifications to the feeders, in conjunction with the sheet control provided by today's vacuum feeders to introduce the sheets into the machine, allow electronics to control lead edge to print register. The electronics not only monitor sheet positioning, but also reject out-of-tolerance sheets.

High Board Line

At about the same time, the equipment manufacturers introduced the high board line. The line of board travel was placed over the operator's head, adding space between the units to accommodate additional equipment such as dryers, sheet cleaners and plate washers. The added space between units added drying time for the inks and improved access. This change in press design allowed for ease of operation and improved efficiencies, including allowing makeready of a new job while another one is in production.

Inks

As equipment manufactures continue to change their press configurations, ink suppliers to the corrugated industry will continually find themselves in the lab reformulating to find the right combination of ink ingredients to match press changes. Interestingly enough, ink companies have gone so far as to place "ink kitchens" in the corrugated facilities. The name itself implies the need to create and modify the ink "recipe" to fit production needs. The ink kitchen also facilitates changing formulas to match conditions and quantities. This has led to a reduction in ink inventories and reduced costs.

Dryers

Dryers have been introduced to help overcome ink dry rate issues resulting from formulations that currently stay open too long on the substrate because they have been slowed down for the air flow from vacuum transfer. Dryers range from IR, hot air and combinations thereof to UV curing systems.

In addition, many of these systems were installed to help produce graphics on coated sheets when roll volumes did not match the substrate. In both of these situations, the dryers, depending on their efficiency, increase production speeds.

UV coatings also provide additional customer appeal and provide a high degree of surface protection to the printed image. This added drying capacity and enhancement of the finished product would not be possible if press manufacturers had not built in additional space between units.

How to Measure Register Without a Ruler

Box A

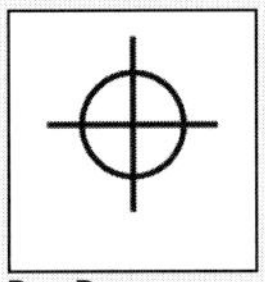

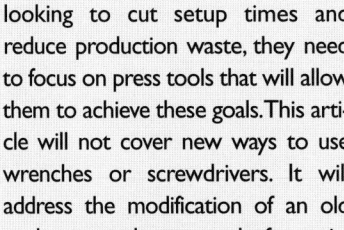

Box B

Example 1. "Traditional" Cross Hair Target

Because companies are continually looking to cut setup times and reduce production waste, they need to focus on press tools that will allow them to achieve these goals. This article will not cover new ways to use wrenches or screwdrivers. It will address the modification of an old tool commonly seen and often misunderstood or poorly utilized in the direct print industry: the common registration target. A modification to this target will allow faster setup times and the reduction of waste.

Looking at **Example 1, Box A**, you will see the "traditional" cross-hair registration target out of register. Box B shows how the target is supposed to look in register. To achieve register, the pressman is required to use a tape measure to evaluate the target and determine how much to move the print. This can lead to poor adjustment as a result of errors in reading the tape.

Example 2, Box A shows a registration target known as the Railroad Track Target, as it resembles the railroad symbol found on most maps, and is where the idea for the target originated. This target will allow you to avoid the use of a tape measure, as it has a "tape measure" built into it. The result is a more efficient and accurate registration process. The objective is to place the triangle on the center line, side-to-side, and through the press direction (laterally and circumferentially). Typically, when this target is used, register adjustments are made only twice to bring the job into register. **Example 2, Box B** shows how the target should look once it is in register.

Using **Example 2, Box A**, take a look at how you evaluate this target. (Note: Decimal numbers have been rounded up.) To adjust the press side to side (laterally, circled in black, **Box A**), you would move:

• Cyan to Black – 1/8-inch or .125-inch or .5mm

• Magenta to Black – 1/64-inch or .016-inch or 6.5mm

• Yellow to Black – 3/32-inch or .094-inch or 1.5mm

To adjust for through-the-press direction (circumferential, circled in blue, **Box A**), you would move:

• Cyan to Black – 3/16-inch or .188-inch or 3.1mm

• Magenta to Black – 3/64-inch or .048-inch or 1.5mm

• Yellow to Black – 7/32-inch or .219-inch or 3mm

These examples are for demonstration only. The lateral and circumferential moves in inches and millimeters will not match proportionally.

Choose the scale and tolerance that fits your equipment. If you are working with inches, you will want to include the conversion table on the printed sheet. This table is valuable for presses working in thousandths of an inch. In some cases, a press may require both fractional and decimal conversion tables. While the conversion chart would appear to take up a lot of space, it is far more convenient to have it on the sheet than taped to the side of a pole in the pressroom.

Design of the Target

You are encouraged to manipulate this target to fit your needs. As you do so, consider the following design elements of the target, as they were refined over several years of testing.

• Line and type point sizes should be chosen from the results of the fingerprint. The longer scale lines above the target's center are representative of the press tolerance. As long as the triangle stays between the lines, you are running at the tolerance of the press. The centerline should extend past the register tolerance lines to allow for their differentiation.

• The triangle is an equilateral triangle equal to the tolerance of the machine. This helps to evaluate the fine adjustment registration, much like a vernier scale. Lines that fit into the centerline are half the length of the centerlines that separate them. The exception to this is at the ends. While this can take up some space on the press

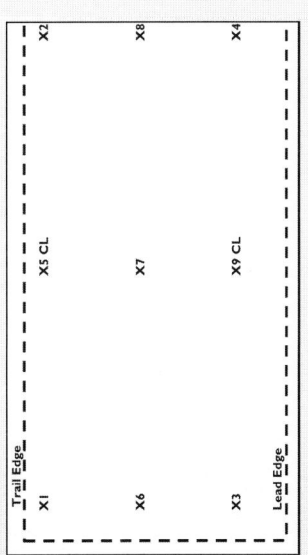

Example 3. Target Configuration

Example 2. Railroad Track Target

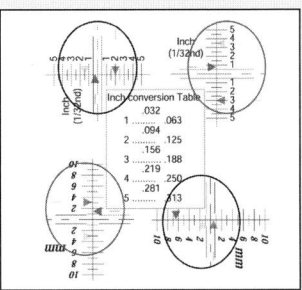

Box A

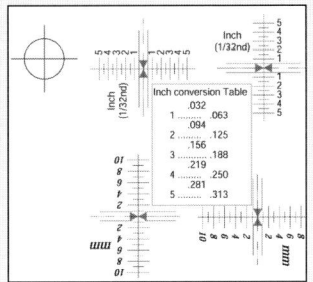

Box B

sheet, this ratio makes it easier for the operator to see when register is achieved. Position the lines that fit into the centerline so they will not fall into the scale or numbers of the target.

• The length of the scale can be adjusted to fit the tolerance you have seen when jobs first print. For example, this lengthening of the scale would be necessary if your cylinders are not zeroed at start-up.

• The target, as described, can easily accommodate up to five colors and can be expanded to more as long as some thought is put into size and location of targets. As you add colors, you will want to consider the color combinations that will be created when the triangles align and how easily they will be seen. As in **Example 2, Box B**, in process work try to have yellow and cyan combine to make green. Put some

thought into this, as confusion could result if spot colors are run that are similar to combined colors.

• For preprint or other types of web printing, this target can be easily adjusted for the gear pitch of the press. If this target will not fit on the web, it can be embedded in the bearer bars.

• The target can also be modified to work with die cutting in- or off-line and to monitor gear slop in the press.

• Lastly, inch and metric scales do not need to be included on the job. Include only the scale that corresponds to the press specifications.

Placing Targets

Now that you know how to use and design the target, where should they be placed? The railroad track targets, along with a traditional cross-hair target, should be placed in the four corners of the printed sheet. A traditional cross hair should be placed in the four centers of the sheet around the perimeter and in the physical center of the press sheet, assuming there is

space. See Examples 3 and 4. Placing targets in these locations will allow the operator to establish the following:

• Position or location of image on the press sheet

• Color-to-color registration

• Square position of the print to the lead edge

Example 3 shows the configuration of registration targets on a typical press sheet. You will note that the Xs form a rectangle. This will allow you to use the traditional register target located in the four corners to ensure that the printed job is square to the lead edge of the sheet. Due to the design of many jobs, location X7 can prove difficult to achieve on many jobs. Include this location when you can fit it on the press sheet.

Example 4 shows how the targets would be placed on the sheet. You will see that the conversion chart can be read from the lead edge, and that the targets form a rectangle. Note: Targets have been enlarged to show position and orientation in this publication.

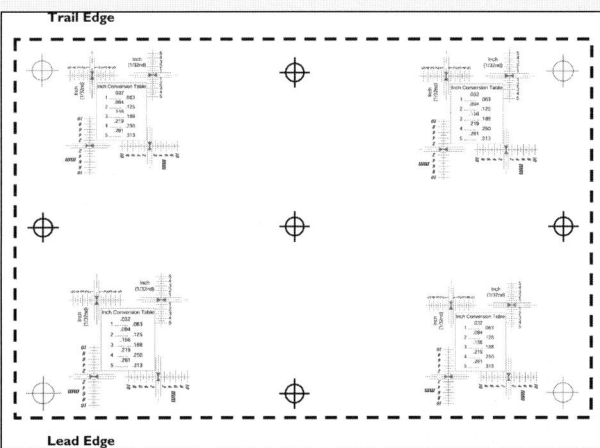

Example 4. Orientation on Sheet

Paper

Product manufacturers are requesting higher-quality graphics to describe the products inside the container. The paper industry has responded by supplying a plethora of liners to match all kinds of situations. This industry has improved its sheet formation and continues to improve the surface qualities of smoothness, whiteness and brightness. The change from the mottle white sheet of 10 years ago to the white top of today has been dramatic.

Paper companies supplying clay-coated sheets to the postprint industry have been faced with their own issues. Printers have requested white, bright and smooth sheets. Clay coating can provide these characteristics; unfortunately, the printer may not have the capability or desire to match anilox volume to the higher-holdout sheet. Consequently, many paper companies have developed coatings that allow some absorption of the ink film and still hold out enough ink on the surface to provide the "shine" desired by the product manufacturer—but at what cost to the process? Many printers who have not matched the anilox volume to the coated sheet are faced with possible reduction in press speeds, the need to add dryers and significant modifications to ink formulas.

Without a strong partnership among all suppliers, the printer is likely to spend a lot of time discovering how to print all over again.

Dust-Cleaning Systems

With the reduction in ink film thickness, dust began to appear in the print. While the lower volumes in anilox rolls improved print fidelity, the volume reduction of the anilox roll decreased the self-washing ability of the previously high-volume systems. Postprint machinery manufacturers responded with devices to clean the sheets, ranging from static or rotating brushes to ionic cleaners with corona curtains. All systems utilized vacuum technology to evacuate displaced dust.

Additional steps have been taken to isolate the printers from dust in corrugated plants by enclosing the press alone in a positive pressure room. With the addition of the rotary die cutter on some high-graphics machines, printing units are being isolated from the die-cutter-generated dust through mechanical means, positive air pressure and vacuum technology around the die cutter.

Chamber-Bladed Systems

The corrugated box industry has made a radical move away from the two-roll system with or without a doctor blade. The arrival of the chamber blade into this market allowed for tighter control of pH and viscosity, and ultimately better control of the ink film on the anilox roll and plate.

The printer—while gaining control over his ink system—no longer has the ability to "cheat" with the inking system, applying more ink to the plate by spreading the gap between the rubber roll and the anilox roll. Consequently, the printer must now learn to truly understand and manage his variables.

Many manufacturers have introduced automatic washup systems for chamber-bladed systems to facilitate fast turnaround. Some also incorporate automatic

viscosity and pH controls. To assist these additions to ink monitoring, ink-temperature control systems have been added, which have allowed operators to spend more time "running" and less time monitoring ink.

Anilox Rolls

While many in the postprint industry still use low-line screen and high-volume rolls, many have moved to higher-line-screen, low-volume rolls to enhance their capabilities of reproducing better images on higher-holdout liners. In the past, an anilox change could take all day and was typically changed only when the roll no longer performed.

For corrugated printers to print higher-quality graphics, they must change their rolls to match the substrate they plan to print. Press manufactures recognized this and created fast-change systems with extra anilox rolls stored in the machine. Through an elevator or turret-type system, one roll can replace another in a matter of minutes with little or no intervention by the operator. With this addition to the press, the postprinter can now run a variety of liners or products on the same machine.

Doctor Blades

The doctor blade has also made significant strides in the past 10 years. This industry has introduced the corrugated printer to steel blades and the resulting benefits to image reproduction.

For those still concerned with safety issues presented by a steel blade, the non-metallic doctor blade industry has delivered new products to the market. Materials have allowed for increased blade molecular weight and wear characteristics with the impregnation of carbon and Teflon. These blades have similar print characteristics to steel.

Automatic Registers & Plate Angling

As the demand for higher quality continues, press manufacturers are installing equipment to monitor quality of production directly on press. One such device monitors register as sheets travel through the machine, adjusts register and rejects out-of-spec sheets, all without intervention. The same system also automatically angles printing plates.

The direct-print industry has come a long way since staples, tape and toothpicks were placed under the lead edge of the carrier to angle the plate. In the future, can

The corrugated press— originally designed to "rotary rubber-stamp" black ink on a brown box— has metamorphosed into a piece of equipment capable of competing with offset labels, laminating and preprint liner.

we expect to find equipment to monitor image quality on sheet-fed corrugated presses? The answer is yes; machinery manufacturers are waiting for better resolutions in video imaging, and for improved speed and accuracy of the traversing cameras.

Plate-Washing Systems

Plate-washing equipment to remove debris from the printing plate continues to be developed. Without these devices, a great deal of time is lost stopping and entering the press to clean the plates.

The design of plate-washing systems runs the gamut of functionality from rotating brushes, water mist and vacuum to a continuously-dampened rag to wipe the plate. These systems allow for cleaning during the run or when sheet-feeding is interrupted.

Independent Drives

The corrugated press of today utilizes independent motors to drive the cylinders. This has enabled press designers to incorporate register on the fly by speeding up or slowing down the unit to lengthen or shorten the print. It has also allowed multiple-plate-thickness packages to be used on the same plate cylinder, independent of the undercut. This system, however, has not yet advanced to the point where multiple plate thicknesses can be used for the same print job.

When you add computer systems and controllers to monitor all the independent drives, you have a machine beginning to resemble rocket science; but there are disadvantages as well as advantages. The computers can now control the setup of impression settings, adjust the paper size, control the inking and washup procedures. The systems also can store settings from a production run and be recalled for a repeat order. In short, computers have made the operator's life easier and press operations more efficient.

These are definite advantages, but must be viewed as assistance to the operation. The operator must constantly question the variables presented and ask if they are the same as the previous run. Blind faith in the machine can cause extensive job difficulties.

The disadvantage is this: The maintenance team must now be mechanics and electronics experts; unfortunately, these skills are not found readily in all facilities.

Plates

The corrugated industry as a whole has finally found the benefits to running thinner plates. While some presses are still manufactured with 0.250-inch undercuts, more and more presses are being built with lesser undercuts. The thinner plates have allowed for better resolution of the graphics on the printed sheet by reducing the dot gain in an image and extending the tonal range.

The industry started with thick plates for a reason: The thick, soft plates allowed distribution of the ink film onto the rough and unlevel surface of the corrugated sheet. While it is true that the thinner plates have increased resolution, solid coverage can become an issue. Effective durometer increases as plates become thinner. This "hardening" of the plate makes it difficult to press the ink into the fibers of the sheet and into the valleys between the flutes. Again, the printer is faced with understanding his variables in order to chose the correct job tooling.

Lastly, digital plates are making headway into the corrugated industry by also providing higher image resolution. The corrugated printer is beginning to reap the benefits of this relatively new plate technology currently enjoyed by other flexo printers.

Prepress

Another group influenced by equipment changes is the industry that creates the images and plates. Prepress workers faced as steep a learning curve as the printers did. For years, this group prepared plates to put black ink on a brown box. Because of all the advancements affecting the corrugated printing industry, many prepress professionals had to relearn their jobs.

This relearning process included a new understanding of control targets (see sidebar), imaging techniques and mounting systems. Transitioning from thick plates to thin meant re-evaluation of exposure times for plates. In order to achieve the desired level of register, production of contiguous plates is now sometimes necessary. This is a significant change from the patchwork of individual pieces sometimes placed on a carrier sheet, often resembling a quilt more than a printing plate.

In order to improve print quality further, foam-supported carrier sheets can be used. The foam-supported carriers under the plates were new to some facilities,

and many discovered that if too much foam is used to build up for high undercuts, registration problems could result.

Not enough can be said about the importance of targets. These tools can provide the press operator with a wealth of information about the production job. Without them, the press operator is like a sighted man in a pitch-black room trying to find the door. He will eventually find it, but not before wasting a lot of time and effort. The job of the prepress house does not stop at placing targets on the print job. The production staff must be educated as to their use and interpretation.

Rotary Die Cutters

Initially, many presses designed to produce high-quality graphics were designed to print only. The conversion of the high-graphics sheet into a corrugated container was reserved for off-line equipment. Current equipment allows for the creation of high-quality graphics and for inline converting.

Once seen as the workhorse of the brown box industry, the new breed of rotary die cutter is a major step toward printing and converting in-line.

Postprinting: A Team Effort

Most flexo printers in industry segments other than corrugated have been working with the innovations discussed in this article for years. For the postprint printer, the last decade has seen more change in this industry than the preceding 10 years. This industry is still changing, and will continue to change. One thing, however, is constant: the importance of identifying your variables, understanding your equipment and being willing to work collectively with all of your suppliers.

The world of higher-quality graphics on corrugated containers is one filled with everyday change and advancements. Those who succeed will not know all the answers, but will be able to identify whom to call, and be willing to make the call and employ the answers given.

About the Author:
Cordes Porcher is technical specialist - high-graphics corrugated for Bobst Group, Corrugated Products, Roseland, NJ. He is a past FLEXO contributor and has also served as an FFTA conference presenter and judge for Excellence in Flexography and Technical Innovation Awards competitions.

SERVO PRESSES

WHAT'S ALL THE FUSS?

By Ken Daming

We have all heard the buzz about servos! They seem to be the most exciting thing going lately. But what are they? What do they do? How are they different from normal motors? What good are they, really? If you find yourself asking these questions, READ ON! I'll try to explain how servo motors are used in a narrow-web press design.

First, here's a short class in Motors 101. There are many different types or classes of motors. Each has applications in which it shines and each has disadvantages. One of the earliest motor designs was the DC (direct current) brushed type. These had simple drives and were inexpensive. The disadvantages were that they were very large in size, had poor low-speed control and were high-maintenance (the motor brushes had to be changed). These motors were used primarily as the main press-drive motor.

DC brushless motors are another class. They are highly efficient, more reliable and less noisy. Obviously, they don't have brushes to replace, but the computer electronics are complex and they cost more than DC brushless motors. Stepper motors are in this class. With a stepper motor, you tell it how far to turn or how many pulses to turn, and it does—or at least you hope it does; there is no feedback. This is a point I'll explore later.

AC (alternating current) induction motors are simple, relatively low-cost and reliable. The disadvantage is that the speed control is expensive, and they can lose some of their speed under a load. On the other hand, AC synchronous motors are small, highly efficient and operate at a constant speed—even under a load. Most servo motors fall into the class of AC synchronous motors.

Servo vs. Stepper Motors

So what is a servo motor? Basically, it is usually an AC motor that has an encoder feedback system. The encoder gives input to the motor drive to tell it what speed the motor is running or what position it is in at all times. These encoders are glass disks with up to 4 million scribe lines that a sensor can see. If you tell the motor to turn a certain amount, the encoder can tell if it turned exactly that amount—and if not, the control system will automatically adjust. This encoder feedback is really the big advantage of a servo motor.

Figure 1. A narrow-web, in-line servo-driven press.

One is able to see from the table that servo motors can have a very high-resolution encoder. This makes them much more accurate than stepper motors. The distinction can be critical. If a servo system is being applied in an application that only requires low resolution and moderate speeds, a stepper may be a better choice. Unfortunately (at least for the time being), servos usually cost more than stepper systems.

Servo Applications

A properly applied servo can increase the accuracy, reliability and flexibility of many press operations. Using a servo in the wrong application is simply a waste of money. There are several applications for which servo motors are a good idea. One is any application that requires a stand-alone drive. Servos are self-contained units. They don't require a drive shaft or some other method of mechanical power transmission. A servo has an advantage in a rewinding or unwinding application because it doesn't put extra load on the line shaft. Servos can also be used in web-pacing applications. They can be tied into a tension transducer to give tension feedback to the motor, and will make the proper speed correction.

A servo has several advantages when driving a plate or

die cylinder. It eliminates the line shaft wrap-up, as well as the gearbox and coupling backlash. When given input by an automatic registry system, the servo can make immediate and accurate registration corrections. This direct tooling drive method is probably the best application for servos. On the other hand, a poor implementation of a servo motor is when all of the mechanical components of the drive line are still contributing to the tooling drive errors (wrap-up, backlash). In addition, the cost of a servo has been added to each station.

Some wide-web CI presses already use servo motors in just about every conceivable location. For instance, they use a servo on the plate roll and another servo on the anilox roll. They use servos when positioning the plate cylinders to achieve proper inking and impression. Some presses use servos as a way to synchronize the speed of the plate cylinder to the impression cylinder so they can perform an off-line job setup without shutting down the press. These are all nice features, but they are expensive.

Comparison of Stepper and Servo Motors	
Stepper Motors	**Servo Motors**
• Low resolution – 2000 steps/rev.	• High resolution – 4 MM steps/rev
• Open Loop – No Feedback	• Closed Loop – encoder feedback
• Often used as a trimming motor	• Stand-alone operation
• Good torque at low speeds	• Good torque at all speeds
• Not good for high speed constant duty	• Will run constantly at high speeds
• Low Cost	• High now, but costs are decreasing

A Look at One Press

Figure 1 shows one example of a narrow-web in-line servo-driven press. It has servo drives on the unwind and rewind. It also has servo drives on the infeed and exit-pacing rollers with tension transducer feedback to accurately control the web tension. Each of the plate and die cylinders is independently servo-driven. The plate cylinder drives the anilox, and the anilox drives the meter roll, so all the gears are loaded in one direction.

The impression roll in this example is idling—not driven at all. Instead, the large-diameter chilling rolls underneath the printing stations are driven all in-line by a line shaft. All of these chill rolls could have also been driven by a servo, but in this example the press manufacturer decided that the benefit of actually driving the web with servos was simply not there. The large diameter of these driven chilling rollers gives the ability to run a wide range of stock without having to change the pacing of the web.

Because servos are driving the plate cylinders and the impression rolls are idling, the operator is able to change the relative speed of the rolls with respect to the web. This is very beneficial when running a thin, unsupported film to eliminate the "snap-back" effect.

Finally, the servo-driven plate cylinders—along with the automatic registration system—give immediate and extremely accurate registration corrections. This is immediately apparent when the stock is changed from one type to another. There is very little web waste because the servos make the plate rolls react so quickly.

The Future of Servos

The servo has already advanced over the last decade into a very reliable system. In the future, the drives will get smaller, faster and less expensive. As communication technology advances, drives will become increasingly integrated. Faster communication will increase the scan and update rates for coordinated multiple axes of servo motors.

Presses will make use of these servo improvements and create increasingly automated setup processes. The fact that servos don't rely on a lineshaft drive will allow an increasing degree of flexibility in various press configurations.

Servo Pros and Cons

In summary, servo motors are very accurate positioning motors. The drives and communication can be synchronized together to operate as though they are one unit. The stand-alone features allow a high degree of flexibility in how the motors—and the components they drive—are configured.

They are somewhat costly now, but the price is coming down. If a servo motor application is implemented properly, it can increase the performance of a press—and maybe even keep the cost the same. If it is not implemented well, it will do nothing but add unnecessary expense to the system.

We are sure to see and hear a lot more about servo drives in the future! 🔃

About the Author...
Ken Daming is the director of product management for Mark Andy Inc., Chesterfield, MO. He can be reached by phone at 636-532-4433 or e-mail: kdaming@markandy.com.

Press Tension

Proper Adjustments Minimize Web Breaks

By Bjorn Olesen

Written into every successful printer's fixed-cost analysis is some allowance for the down time caused by web breaks on the press. Estimates put the figure at anything from 15 minutes to one hour (or 100,000 impressions). Wise printers and converters should invest in web-break detection and containment devices that monitor and even shut down the machine when a break occurs.

A good tension control system and a thorough maintenance program are two of the prerequisites for continuous uninterrupted process throughput. Research carried out in the United States has shown that the issue of maintenance is more important than people realized. In instances where some routine maintenance had been skipped, there was a corresponding rise in web breaks. Poorly maintained and even inappropriate web-control equipment played a significant role.

In some instances, the pattern of web breaks suggested substrate problems, which were eventually traced back to the material supplier. In another well-documented case, repeated web breaks were caused by construction taking place in the plant and distracting the operators.

There are also a number of little things that can contribute to web breaks. There is the last-hours-of-the-shift syndrome, when operators are not working at their best. There is also the running-in period when a new job or an inexperienced operator takes control. Some of these problems can be attended to with training or altered work patterns.

Accurate press tension measurement makes it possible to compensate for the physical inconsistencies of difficult materials. It helps to reduce web scrap and allows a process to run at higher speeds with defect-free output. Also, it plays a role in minimizing the risk of web breaks, one of the most hotly debated subjects in printing and converting. Tension control facilitators should be examined and, if suspect, replaced with modern alternatives.

Press Tension Zones

Tension is sometimes used to correct web-handling problems. For example, the web may have a loose edge, so the machine operator endeavors to increase tension to stretch the web and eliminate the looseness. Alternatively, the web may not track properly through the machine; so, again, tension is increased to correct the problem. This usage of tension as a quick fix creates still more problems, though, such as web breakage, stretching, wrinkling and print length variations. Therefore, it is recommended that instead, the source of the initial web-control problem be tackled directly.

Typically, the flexographic press has more than one tension zone. This is because the process in any individual zone may require a different tension level or pattern than the processes in other zones.

A press tension zone is that length of web that extends from one tension-affecting device to the next. Typical tension-affecting devices are: unwind or rewind core shaft with attached motor, brake or clutch; driven rolls; braked rolls; nip rolls where at least one roll is driven or braked; or any other device that may add or subtract tension to or from the web.

Unwind Tension Zone. Tension levels should be equal to or less than the tension in the wind-up roll. Excessive tension can cause the roll to tighten on itself and telescope. This is most noticeable when processing smooth or slippery webs. Extensible webs such as polyethylene and unsupported vinyl are run with much lower tension than non-extensible webs such as paper or foil.

Unwind tension control is necessary for good registration. This is especially true on stack-type presses as well as CI (central impression) presses. Sufficient unwind web tension must be applied to maintain an even flow of material into the printing section. Further, the tension value must not be so high that it causes slippage in the infeed draw roll section, or so low that there is not sufficient tension to properly track the web.

In the unwind braking system, the braking power is decreased as the material unwinds from full roll to core to maintain the desired web tension. A controlling device such as a dancer or load cell may be used to regulate the brake. The basic purpose of the braking system is to apply just enough holdback force to the

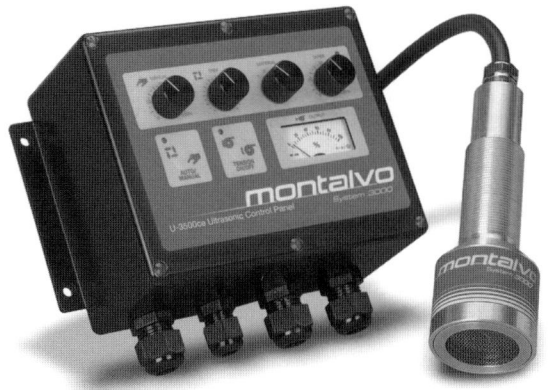

> *A good tension control system and a thorough maintenance program are two prerequisites for continuous uninterrupted process throughput.*

expiring roll to maintain a constant tension into the printing section.

Intermediate Zone. Constant tension is equally desirable in the intermediate zone. The process, the web material, its thickness and width usually determine the correct tension. Extensible films must be run with low tension to prevent stretching, the usual cause of short print lengths and of curling upon release of tension.

Rewind Zone. In the rewind zone, either constant or tapered tension is used. The selection is determined by factors such as the web material, the build-up ratio (full roll diameter divided by core diameter) and the tension capability of the rewind drive. Usually, build-up ratios of more than 5:1 require taper, which is a tension profile having less tension at the full roll than at the core. Slippery webs are normally wound with a higher taper, while extensible webs are wound with low taper or constant tension. Webs requiring high tension and large build-up ratios need high taper to keep from exceeding the capability of the rewind drive.

Load Cell Tension Control

The only method of tension control that displays a true and accurate measurement of tension – and offers a display of "actual" tension – is the load cell. In addition, load cells are a relatively low-cost investment that provides a quick return on capital investment. They should be placed at strategic positions.

Load cells are highly accurate, and increasingly play an integral role in "closed loop" web control systems. Used in conjunction with amplifier modules and a controller, the system automatically compensates for such tension-affecting factors as changes in speed, diameter, web characteristics, brake fade, etc.

The load cell system tension control is generally either full-control or tension-trim. Full-control systems have torque outputs, which are determined by the load cell signal. If tension is very low compared with set tension, the controller will increase tension output. Conversely, if tension is very high, the opposite will occur. This type of control is used on unwinds and rewinds but not in an intermediate position.

Tension-trim is used at the intermediate zone. The load cell signal varies the motor, clutch or brake torque within a narrow band. Another signal—usually speed—determines the operating signal. The load cell signal allows the system to control tension rather than overspeed (as in a draw system) and, unlike a draw system, will automatically compensate for variations in speed, drive accuracy and web thickness to maintain proper tension.

Yet another type of tension trim is used on rewinds. The load cell signal is again used to control torque within a narrow band, but roll diameter as well as speed determines the operating torque.

No Single Solution

Apart from maintaining a regular maintenance program and ensuring tension-control equipment is performing well, there are ways to reduce the risk of web breaks. For instance, evaluate the material storage area. A surprising number of printers/converters don't use any atmospheric controls in their storage areas. Ideally, you should have at least some form of ambient temperature control, a humidity indicator and dust control.

It is also useful to do some monitoring. If web breaks are occurring frequently, collect some process data. Even such basic information as the type of machine, the machine speed, the area where the web breaks occur and the type of substrate being run can reveal some surprising facts.

There is no single solution to the problem of web breaks. Each new job and machine throws another set of variables into the equation. Web breaks will probably never be a thing of the past, because the causes are too diverse. We can, however, minimize the risks.

About the author...
Bjorn Olesen is managing director of Danarota Technic A/S, the European manufacturing and marketing division of the Montalvo Corp., headquartered at Bjert in Jutland Denmark.

REREGISTER SYSTEMS

OPPORTUNITIES GROW WHEN PRINTERS REREGISTER PREPRINTED MATERIALS

By Joe A. Nicholson

Fictitious Label Company is in a tough situation. One of its best customers has just announced that its new label will integrate several existing labels into one. The customer wants Fictitious Label to do the press work. This should be a good thing for Fictitious, almost doubling its business from this customer.

To produce the job requires 10 print stations. Fictitious Label's presses have only six. The label company has no immediate plans to invest in a larger press, nor can it justify such a purchase for this job alone. The company does not want to lose this customer. What should Fictitious Label do?

One solution is to produce the job with a reregister system. Reregister, sometimes referred to as insetting or reinsertion, is a means of registering preprinted material back through a printing press or finishing equipment for a second pass of printing or converting. One of the easiest ways of thinking of reregister capabilities is to look at your press, then imagine it having two of everything. Doubling a press's capability is one of many benefits of a reregister system.

Principles of Reregister

Knowing the basic principles of reregister systems will help you understand how it has evolved into a flexible piece of equipment offering multiple benefits to the user.

Reregister systems have been in existence for more than 20 years. They are used in many market segments, including business forms, direct mail, envelopes, flexible packaging, labels, publications and tags. Like many print technologies, the reregister system has developed into a highly accurate and easy-to-use machine. In general, reregister systems can be broken into two main categories: direct and indirect.

A direct system controls the tool position, such as a print or die station, to the web position. The system phases a cylinder in the press to be in register with the running preprinted material. A direct system can be the best choice for certain applications, but it has a disadvantage that the indirect system does not have: Each tool must be controlled by its own system.

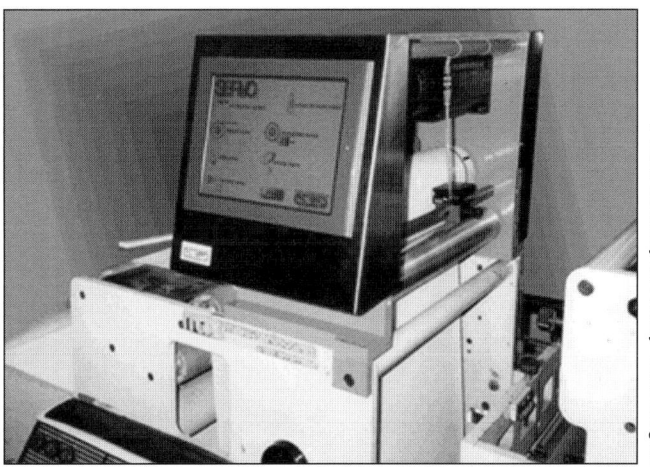

Portable reregister system mounted on a Mark Andy press.

Photo courtesy of Rotary Technologies

An indirect system controls the preprinted web position to the press position. Just as each print and die station in a press is synchronized by its own drive train, with an indirect system the preprinted material is synchronized to the entire press. This is what makes the indirect system so flexible: One system can keep the preprinted material in register to multiple print or die stations. The focus of this article is the indirect system.

How It Works

For any reregister system to work, it must know at all times the press position and the preprinted web position. Usually an encoder is belt- or gear-driven from the press. An encoder can feed the press's rotation and position data to the system. This data represents press position.

A color-mark sensor is used to read the preprinted material. The data from the encoder is compared to this signal. That data represents the preprint web position.

Typically, the press's infeed pacing cylinder—the cylinder that controls web tension—is then used to synchronize these two positions. There is usually a large wrap around the cylinder that is nipped to the cylinder by a rubber roller to prevent web slippage. Many times, the cylinder is coated to achieve high traction. By changing the speed of the infeed cylinder in relation to press speed, the system is actually changing the position of the preprint material in relation to the press.

An easy way of picturing how a reregister system works is by imagining the infeed cylinder feeding the preprint material into the press so that every time a print mark is sensed, the plate roll is at 90 degrees; this is considered perfect register. Suddenly a print mark is sensed when the plate roll is at 89 degrees. The preprinted material is now running faster than the

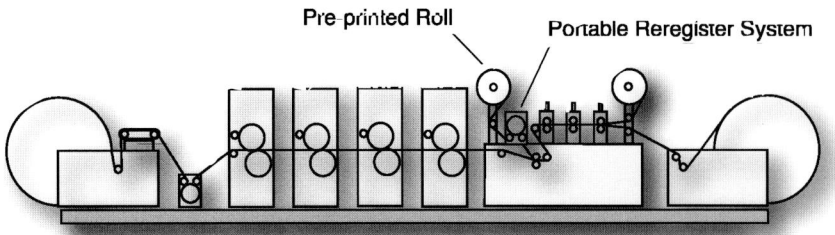

Pre-printed Roll — Portable Reregister System

press, so the system slows down the infeed cylinder to restore register.

A faster-running infeed will advance the web, whereas a slower-running infeed will retard the web. This ability to speed up or slow down the infeed cylinder independent of the speed of the press is the control for reregistration. The better the control, the more accurate the system.

Servo Motors Improve System

Some of the first press installations were difficult, compared to today's standards. While many press models had a variable-speed infeed—which works great for its intended purpose of adjusting and maintaining web tension—they lacked the high precision and immediate response time necessary for reregistration control.

In this case, a precision speed-correcting gearbox, such as a planetary or harmonic differential, together with a correction motor had to be retrofitted onto the press. This involved re-engineering the press's drive train from the main drive shaft to the infeed cylinder.

The use of gearless technology changed all this. An AC servo motor can independently drive the infeed cylinder; provide exceptional control for reregistration, with accuracy measured in thousandths of an inch. With a servo motor, the reregister system does not have to be mechanically tied to the press. This makes a portable reregister system possible.

Portable Systems

Portability has greatly increased the value of a reregister system. The ability to move the system to any number of presses has eased job scheduling. It enables users to find more creative uses of the system than just adding more colors to the press.

Unlike its fixed-installed predecessor, a portable system does not necessarily have to be mounted just after the unwinder. Some users are mounting the system down the press line in order to introduce a second preprinted web in register to the one currently being printed for multi-web constructed products.

Off-line finishing is another great use for the portable system. Some jobs require the press to run at slower speeds due to, for example, the use of a special die cutter or sheeting die. The portable reregister system could be mounted on a die cutter designed to produce blank label stock. The job could be printed roll-to-roll at a higher press speed, then finished on the die cutter. This could quickly free the higher-overhead press for the next job.

In order to reregister accurately, the system must have extreme control of the infeed cylinder. This means the reregister system is also a terrific infeed pacing system for web tension. A servo-driven infeed pacing system is currently state-of-the-art. It is proven to control tension and improve color-to-color registration on substrates never intended to be run on certain presses, such as unsupported films. When the portable system is not being used for reregistration, it can be used full-time on any number of presses as an infeed pacing system.

Have you ever seen several rolls—or, for that matter, several pallets of rolls—printed, only to find out they were all missing a line of type? A reregister system can also be a salvage system to repair rolls that would otherwise be thrown away.

The portable reregister system has truly become a flexible piece of equipment that offers many benefits for its users. The system can add colors, introduce second preprinted webs in register, do off-line finishing, serve as an infeed pacing system and can even repair mistakes.

About the Author...
Joe A. Nicholson is technical director for Rotary Technologies, Orlando, FL, a leading manufacturer of web-control equipment and supplies for the printing and converting industries. For more information about the company or reregister systems, call 407-888-2886 or email info@rotarytechnologies.com.

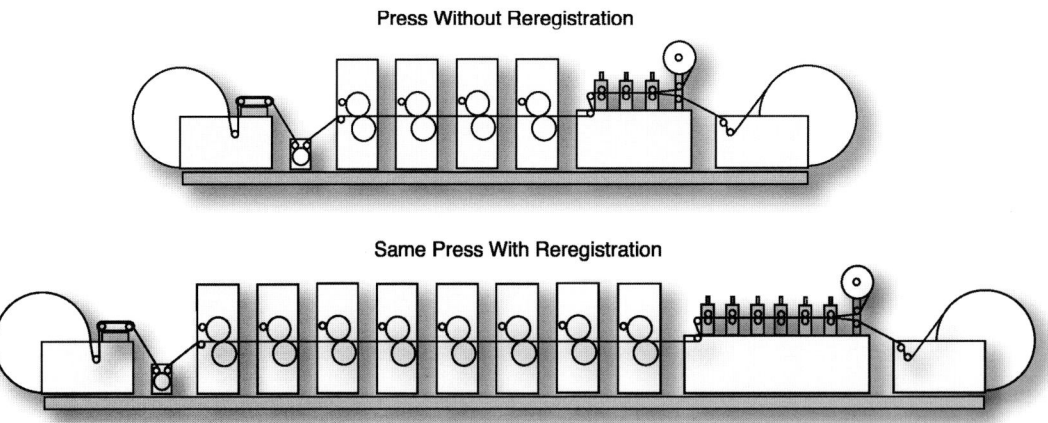

Press Without Reregistration

Same Press With Reregistration

BETWEEN-COLOR DECK DRYERS

REGULAR MAINTENANCE IS CRITICAL TO PRESS OPERATION

By Gary Schollmeyer

Between-color deck dryers (also called interstation dryers) on the press play an intricate role in the printing process, yet they are often overlooked and improperly maintained. If the dryers are not properly balanced and maintained, excessive waste and machine downtime can result.

The purpose of the between-color deck dryers is to remove a sufficient amount of volatiles from the ink so that each print station may apply another color without altering the previous one. Depending on the age and the manufacturer of the press, ideally you want a separate supply fan and exhaust fan for the between-deck dryers and main tunnel oven. This way, the operator can independently control the temperature of the air that goes to the between-deck dryers and the air that goes to the main tunnel ovens.

Higher air temperature means faster drying time. The greater the volume of heated air directed toward the substrate, the quicker the volatiles can be vaporized. High temperatures can also have drawbacks, such as substrate damage and swelling of the central impression drum. The main thing to consider is that air dries, and heat assists in drying.

In most cases, the supply fan takes the air from either the roof or inside the plant, runs it through a gas-fired burner and directs it to the between-color dryers and the main tunnel dryer. The heated air is pushed onto the substrate through air nozzles running across the between-color deck dryers. This vaporizes the volatiles.

The exhaust fan then pulls the air out and sends it either into the atmosphere

> **The purpose of the between-color deck dryers is to remove a sufficient amount of volatiles from the ink so that each print station may apply another color without altering the previous one.**

or into a pollution-control incinerator device. To keep harmful solvent fumes out of the pressroom, the exhaust volume should be greater than the supply volume. When dealing with dryer exhaust rates, consult the press manufacturer or the dryer manufacturer.

Maintenance Guidelines

Improperly balanced dryers can lead to dirty print, premature staining of anilox rolls, ghosting, trapping and the reduction of solvent capture, among other consequences. You can prevent these

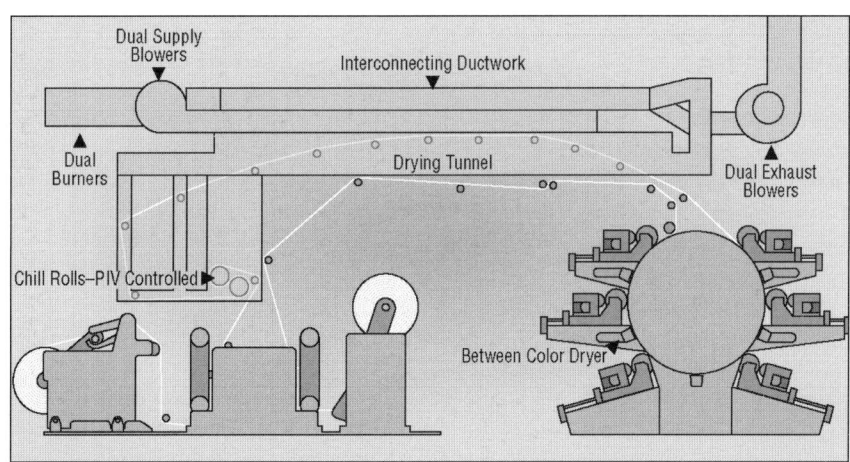

A typical dryer system on a central-impression press. There are individual dryers between each print station except the last one.

On a central-impression press, a between-color (also called interstation) dryer is located between each print station. Photo courtesy of Mark Andy/Comco.

problems by following some recommended preventive maintenance guidelines.

First, make a complete inspection of the blower units, paying close attention to belts, proper lubrication and any debris inside the motor cage that can be removed. Next, clean the screens. Some presses have a central screen collection catch. The screen and or screens should be removed from this area and properly cleaned. A few of the older-model printing presses have a screen built into the exhaust hose. In some cases, the only way to see this screen is by shining a flashlight down the supply hose. The screen should be removed, properly cleaned and reinstalled.

Take the between-color dryer barrels off of the press, paying close attention not to damage any equipment, such as the central impression drum, anilox rolls or printing cylinders. As each dryer is removed, a reference number should be punched into it to ensure that the dryer is reinstalled in the same deck it was taken from.

Once the dryer is removed, it should be properly cleaned to make sure all the vent holes are free of any debris and ink. Pay close attention to the ends of the dryers. Any ink build-up can cause web breaks, as well as wear on the central impression drum. Once this is achieved, the dryers can be reinstalled.

Each between-color dryer hose should be inspected for holes, ink and debris that may have built up inside. Replace the hoses as necessary; this is inexpensive, due to the fact most between-color dryer hoses are short in length.

Once all the above is achieved, and the dryers are reinstalled, the outfeed exhaust baffle should be completely opened. (The baffle adjustments should have a directional arrow to indicate closed and open positions.) One person with a smoke stick or smoke gun should slowly move the smoke from one end of the dryer to the other while a second person slowly opens the air-intake baffle until the smoke starts exhausting through the between-color dryer.

Then mark the baffle adjustments to each dryer and tighten down. This will give you a reference as to where you had them adjusted, in case the adjusters are moved. Keep in mind that too much exhausting will create negative airflow around the printing deck area.

The maintenance steps outlined above should be performed on a regularly scheduled basis once or twice a year. Once implemented, these practices can reduce valuable press downtime as well as print defects.

About the Author:
Gary Schollmeyer is customer support specialist for All Printing Resources, Glendale Heights, IL.

A typical dryer airflow scheme.

BUILDING ANILOX PERFECTION

UNDERSTANDING THE ANILOX ROLL MANUFACTURING PROCESS

By Dan Foy

Much discussion and marketing have been devoted to laser-engraving technology, depth-to-opening ratios, cell shapes available and other themes regarding anilox rolls. All are very important topics; but how many printers, production supervisors, production managers, purchasing managers and co-suppliers have a basic understanding of the construction and processing of the anilox roll itself?

A lot of time and money are spent on anilox rolls, yet it is amazing how little those who use, manage and purchase anilox roll inventories every day know about them.

This article will follow the procedure that every high-quality anilox roll goes through during the manufacturing process, from incoming inspection to final inspection. We will discuss the "how's" and "why's" of proper anilox roll manufacturing and reconditioning.

Incoming Inspection

Every anilox roll base, whether new or reconditioned, is subject to an incoming inspection process, which qualifies the base for manufacturing.

Before we inspect the roll itself, the shipping container is evaluated for damage and suitability for re-use, repair or disposal. Damaged shipping containers are a tip-off to possible structural damage, on our receiving dock and yours!

Every exterior dimension of the anilox roll is documented, including outside diameter, bearing surface diameter, face length, taper and total indicated run-out (TIR) tolerances. How do we know what the dimensions are supposed to be? In most cases, we have blueprints with OEM (original equipment manufacturer) dimensions and tolerances, as the printer should for dimensional ref-

During incoming inspection, the physical dimensions and condition of both new bases and reconditioned rolls are evaluated.

erence. But there are times—due to modifications or older presses—when we have to CAD a print ourselves and rely on customer-supplied information for correct dimensions.

One critical internal dimension the inspector has the ability to measure, using an ultrasonic depth gauge, is wall thickness of rolls constructed of tubing. If the roll should subsequently require a diameter restoration (buildup) and the wall falls short of minimum thickness required, we are restricted in our restoration method and can only provide a buildup that is non-reusable. If, however, the wall thickness is .700-inch or greater and the roll has proper overall size, a welding method is used. This renders the roll reusable, saving tremendous buildup costs in the future.

New bases that pass the incoming inspection process go directly to Second Machining for a light cut to prepare the surface for the ceramic application operation, while reconditioned rolls remain at First Machine awaiting disposition.

First Machine

Having inspected and qualified the roll base from the outside, it is time to discover how the roll was previously constructed. An anilox roll can be reconditioned several times and may be making the transition from mechanically-engraved chrome or ceramic to laser-engraved ceramic. Some may be chrome gravure cylinders, while others arrive as used laser-engraved ceramic and will be reprocessed as the same.

What's underneath the chrome or ceramic exterior? We don't know until the machinist performs an "end-cut assessment," during which the roll is set up in a lathe and a cutting tool is used to remove the outer layers down to the original core. This cut is typically less than 1/2-inch long at the end of the roll. In the case of a mechanically-engraved cylinder, the machinist will likely encounter copper, monel and other soft, metallized materials used for mechanical engraving.

Regardless of the outcome of the incoming inspection and first machining, all findings are documented and the report is sent to the Customer Service Department. Based on the findings of the report, the customer can be contacted and told what it will take to recondition the roll, how long it will take and what it will cost.

In some cases, it is more expensive to recondition the existing roll than to purchase a new base. The choice is the customer's to make. Some narrow-web bases are very inexpensive, and inventories are maintained by the anilox roll manufacturer. These are considered disposable.

If the base is found to be mechanically sound and the customer proceeds with the reconditioning process, the machinist will remove the balance of the chrome, ceramic and any metallized buildup and remove .005-inch of the original core.

Any anilox roll manufacturer who re-uses any metallized or porous buildup material runs the risk of processing a contaminated roll, which may likely "blister" or de-laminate the ceramic coating.

Grit Blast

Following the initial machining process, the roll surface is prepared to receive either metallized buildup, welded buildup or plasma-applied materials by being subjected to a chemical cleaning followed by severe blasting process with a coarse blast medium. The purpose of this operation is twofold:

- Remove any potential contamination/oxidation from the core, which may prove fatal to a successful coating process.

- Provide additional surface area for successive materials to adhere to, by "roughing-up" the machined surface. After the first machining process, anilox rolls will proceed on one of two paths:

- Following the initial machining process, material has been removed and size has been lost. This needs to be replaced; therefore, size restoration or buildup is required.

- First machining requires the removal of only the ceramic coating and minimal base material; therefore, no formal buildup is required to restore roll size. This is referred to as a "skim-cut." The roll proceeds directly to the plasma ceramic operation.

Metallizing or Welded Buildup

It stands to reason that if a significant amount of material is removed from the roll diameter during the First Machine operation, then this material or diameter needs to be restored in order for the roll to function properly in the press. This is due to the fact that ceramic materials alone have thickness limitations. Depending on the size and the construction of the anilox roll core, the printer and manufacturer have a couple of options to reconstruct this dimension. The basic options are to either "spray" or to "weld" the materials by one of two methods. We will explore the basics of these operations.

Metallizing is the process of restoring the outside diameter of a cylinder by applying metal in wire form to a heat source, which in turn melts the wire and applies the melted material via a high-pressure stream of air. These systems are either electric or gas-

An "end-cut assessment" discloses materials previously applied to an anilox roll. Materials typically under ceramic and chrome surfaces include copper, aluminum bronze, aluminum, mild steel or stainless steel.

The electric arc spray process applies melted metals to the anilox roll diameter to restore size and to repair bearing surfaces where needed.

A welded buildup process is used to restore anilox roll diameter. Materials available are mild and stainless steel, for corrosive environments.

fired systems in which the metallizing gun traverses the cylinder as it rotates, insuring consistent coverage side-to-side and around the circumference of the cylinder. There are four basic materials used in the metallizing process. Each has an appropriate application:

- Aluminum bronze: simply a filler material to replace size; very machineable.

- Mild steel: most bases are mild steel; can be used to repair bearing surfaces.

- Stainless steel: applied where corrosive-resistant properties are required.

- Aluminum: restores size to light-weight bases constructed of aluminum.

Metallizing is capable of restoring roll diameters up to .180-inch. Beyond this amount, the process may not be practical.

This method of roll-diameter restoration is suitable for most roll sizes and configurations. Despite the versatility and comparatively low cost of this process, future re-conditionings cannot and should not re-use any of the metallized buildup material. The reason for this is that the ceramic coating is porous and so are the metallized buildups; therefore, they are potentially contaminated after exposure to inks and cleaning chemistry and must be stripped off completely. Even localized damage requires that the entire surface be removed completely in order to eliminate possible contamination.

A welded buildup, as the name implies, is the process of restoring roll diameter by means of a specialized welding process that utilizes metal in wire form, an inert gas and electricity to melt the wire and deposit

The second machining process removes excess buildup materials on a conventional engine lathe to provide a mechanically sound base for plasma spray application of ceramic and bond materials.

the material around the circumference of the cylinder. Welded buildups can be processed with either mild or stainless steel. Stainless steel provides corrosive-resistant properties where needed, as in the metallized buildup.

In extreme cases, where the cylinder is actually submerged in a corrosive material, a manufacturer who understands the application will recommend a stainless-steel core. This is very expensive but well worth the price compared to the cost of reconditioning blistered mild-steel bases.

The welded buildup process is reserved for wide-web anilox roll cores due to the extreme heat generated during this process. Smaller cores are susceptible to structural distortion, which would destroy the integrity of the core, which is vital for a precision metering instrument.

Though the cost is generally higher than that of a metallized buildup, the welded coating is 100-percent dense and has a metallurgical bond to the original base; thus, it can be repaired and re-used on successive reconditioning(s) even for localized damage, saving significant dollars on future reconditions.

Second Machining

During the course of the entire manufacturing process, the base goes on a roller-coaster ride of under-size to over-size at least twice. Here at Second Machining, we are at one of the peaks of the ride and are oversize following the application of the appropriate buildup material. Some cores arrive at this operation directly from First Machine because they do not require buildup. New cores arrive slightly oversize.

Second machining is a turning operation on an engine lathe and is extremely critical to the production of a mechanically-sound base because it is the last opportunity to guarantee that the core itself is straight and true. In other words, proper dimensional taper and TIR are two crucial dimensions to a precise anilox roll; they determine the transfer of consistent ink films across the face of the roll and around the circumference.

Second machining will reduce the roll diameter to allow room for the upcoming plasma application of barrier and ceramic coatings.

Plasma application utilizes a combination of gasses to achieve temperatures as high as 24,000 degrees Fahrenheit to melt powdered materials for a subsonic ride to the surface of the anilox roll. Desirable surface qualities are high hardness and low porosity levels. Scheduled metallurgical testing assures quality applications.

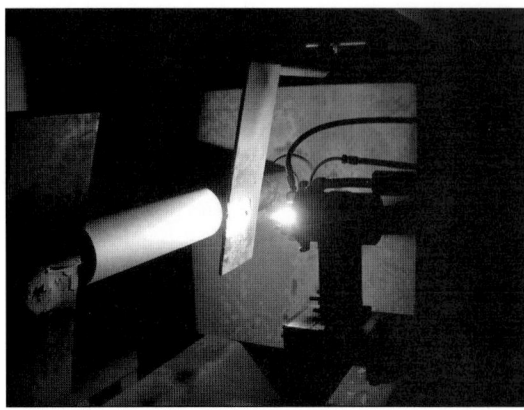

Plasma Coating

The plasma coating stage is the point at which a corrosive-resistant barrier and the ceramic coatings are applied. At this time, the core has been either skim-cut or built up and turned down to accommodate the thickness of the combined plasma coatings. It then must be chemically cleaned and grit-blasted a second time.

The application involves the introduction of powdered materials to a 20,000-degree ionized gas stream (plasma) that melts the powder to semi-liquid form and applies it under extreme pressure to the roll surface. As in the metallizing phase, the plasma gun traverses the roll length as it rotates, applying a uniform coating thickness around the circumference and from side to side.

The first material to be applied is a barrier of corrosive-resistant material, which under printing applications is adequate protection from inks, cleaners and other pressroom chemicals. The thickness of this material can vary, but is no less than 0.010-inch.

Following application of the corrosive-resistant barrier material, the ceramic coating is added. Like a printer applying ink as efficiently as possible, the anilox roll manufacturer wishes to apply a minimum thickness of ceramic coating. Different screen counts and engraving depths require different ceramic coating thicknesses. For example, an 800-line screen engraving with a cell depth of 8 microns does not require the thickness needed for a 120-line screen at a depth of 60 microns.

The materials and the application process are very expensive. Excess material applied is wasted because when properly reconditioned, all porous materials on or within the roll structure must be removed to eliminate the possibility of reconditioning over a contaminated surface. This includes ceramic, corrosive-resistant barrier material (if present) and any metallized buildup material.

Superfinishing

Having applied the plasma coatings, we are left with a surface that is too rough to engrave and larger than the finished outside diameter.

This ceramic-coated surface is used for two-roll coating and basic printing applications where consistent film thickness is not critical. The raw surface roughness achieves volumes ranging from 6.0 to 8.0 BCM around the circumference and end to end. Grind and laser finishing processes are used to refine volumes for more consistent ink films for applications incorporating doctor-blade systems for higher-quality print. Significantly less expensive than a formally laser-engraved anilox roll, this surface offers the benefits of a ceramic-coated roll at or near the cost of a chrome finish.

Measuring a surface roughness of 220 Ra (too rough to be engraved), this surface is subjected to a grinding process utilizing CNC grinding technology. A grinding wheel impregnated with industrial diamonds is used to remove excess size and smooth the surface to a 20 to 30 Ra while maintaining a straight and true base.

"Ra" or "roughness average" is a common unit of measure used to compare the relative smoothness or roughness of a surface. The smaller the Ra number, the smoother the finish. These values are measured with instruments that drag a stylus across the surface to be measured or by interferometric measurement systems using reflected light.

Grinding dimensionally stabilizes the ceramic coating to precision tolerances that cannot be produced by machining alone. Circularity, size consistency from end to end (taper), concentricity and TIR are addressed in the grinding process.

Still too rough to engrave, the roll is then polished with diamond-impregnated stones and diamond-impregnated paste, with diamond particle size descending from large to small sizes. The anilox roll

During the Super Finish CNC Grinding Operation, the sprayed ceramic coating is taken from a surface roughness of over 200 Ra to approximately 30 Ra. The surface is then polished down to an Ra value less than 10 with diamond impregnated stones, diamond impregnated paste and honing oil.

rotates as these stones polish the roll to a roughness measurement of 4 to 6 Ra and the correct diameter, prior to laser engraving.

At the Superfinish stage, the roll diameter may be less than that of the finished O.D. (outside diameter) due to the fact that in the laser-engraving process (CO2 laser application only), the roll diameter will increase in size. The deeper the cell, the greater the increase in size.

Laser Engraving

Having prepared a mechanically sound base with appropriate materials and processes, the super-finished anilox roll is now ready for the laser engraving process. After reviewing the shop order for proper engraving specifications, the laser operator will load the anilox roll into the laser bed using the appropriate configuration of "chuck and center" or "chuck and chuck" to hold the anilox roll in place.

Using precision measuring instruments, the laser operator will verify the measurements taken at the Superfinish operation for O.D. and taper. Using a dial indicator, the ceramic surface of the anilox roll will be indicated to within 0.0005-inch of running perfectly true to the bearing surfaces.

Having been polished to a surface roughness smoother than a mirror, the ceramic surface is ready for the laser engraving process. Before engraving the entire surface, laser technicians perform "test-burns" to ensure accuracy and consistency of laser operating conditions, similar to a printer performing a press check of a live job to ensure quality at the start of a pressrun.

Dead bands or non-engraved bands at the ends of the anilox roll may be laid out. Dead bands are primarily used to provide a smooth surface for end seals to ride against, in order to seal efficiently while providing longer life to the seals.

Accuracy and consistency are the keys to an efficient anilox roll inventory and flexographic printing process. With this in mind, the laser operator enters the parameters into the computer that operates the laser system. Now, just because the operator provides the correct information to the computer, that does not guarantee that the laser will do exactly what it is told! Why? Because one of the shortcomings of CO2-powered laser systems is that they are extremely maintenance-intensive. With many moving parts, lenses that lose focus and variables such as atmospheric conditions, lasers require continuous maintenance.

How do we live with this relative inconsistency? The operator performs what are called "test-burns," in which the laser beam is engaged for a very short period of time at the end of each roll to ensure the accuracy and quality of the engraving. If the engraving is accurate (i.e., has the correct volume) and meets quality standards for cell shape, then the entire roll can be engraved. If not, adjustments can be made to the laser system to correct the shortcomings of the engraving before completing the entire roll. Test burns are inspected with a gravure microscope and measured with an interferometric measurement system. The procedure is similar to a printer performing a press check of a live job to ensure quality at the start of a pressrun.

Once the laser engraving process is begun, actual engraving time is a function of surface area, screen count, volume requirements and laser hardware being employed. Larger anilox rolls require longer engraving times, based on shear size. The smallest anilox rolls, such as those used in hand-proofing systems, require only several minutes (not including setup time), while the largest rolls used in the corrugated and coating industries take many hours.

Higher-screen-count anilox rolls generally require more time due to the exponentially increasing number of cells per square inch, while engravings at the high-volume end of the engraving spectrum—20 - 70 BCM—require more blasts of the laser to sculpt out their massive openings.

This article focuses on CO2-powered laser systems, but must mention the use of solid-state laser systems known as Nd:YAG lasers. The appropriate application of this process based on practical testing is for extremely high screen counts (1200 – 1800) at relatively high volumes (2 - 4 BCM), for use with UV inks. Engraving times are comparable, given that the YAG is engraving more cells per square inch.

After the engraving process is completed, the roll will receive a finely-applied polish with diamond or other abrasive materials, depending on line screen. This process removes any unwanted "casted" ceramic left over from the laser burn. If left unchecked, the casting (or "recast," as it is known) can prematurely wear doctor blades and plates. When properly engraved, cell walls are smooth with little to no recast. The laser operator will inspect and measure the engraving at a number of points, determined by the anilox roll width, and document these on a cell-volume inspection report.

To minimize the handling of the laser-engraved surface and to guarantee the accuracy of the laser

When the anilox roll is properly crated, the laser-engraved ceramic surface is isolated from the interior of the crate for shipping. Exposed journals are sprayed with a rust-inhibitive material to protect the exposed steel surfaces during shipping and storage.

Following final inspection, during which critical dimensions and tolerances are verified, the ceramic surface is wrapped in a layer of foam-backed paper, a layer of corrugated stock as well as protective rubber bands that prevent chipping on the ends of the roll.

engraver's measurements, all engraved anilox rolls are subjected to a second inspection and measurement process. Referred to as Engraving Q.C., the engraving is again inspected for geometric cell quality and cosmetic flaws, and is measured for accuracy within the volume tolerance. If the engraving measures within acceptable tolerance levels (which can be as low as +/- 4 percent) and is within acceptable variation, a microphotograph is taken under appropriate magnification, which will appear on the Quality Certification Report.

Upon successful inspection and measurement, the anilox roll moves on to the final inspection stage. If the engraved surface contains any cosmetic flaws or fails to measure within acceptable tolerances the roll will be rejected and reprocessed.

Final Inspection

Despite the fact that all dimensions of the anilox roll have been monitored throughout the manufacturing process, the final inspection process will revalidate all dimensions of the anilox roll except for the engraving. All dimensions will meet or exceed OEM (original equipment manufacturer) specifications to ensure anilox roll performance.

Critical dimensions that are measured and documented at Final Inspection are total Indicated runout (TIR), outside diameter/ taper and bearing surface diameters. Other

parts of the anilox roll inspected are threaded holes, keyways, bored holes, chamfers and journal steps. A visual inspection of the engraved surface under inspection lighting will eliminate the chance of a cosmetically flawed surface being shipped to a customer.

Upon completion of the final inspection process, the inspector will wrap the engraved surface with a layer of foam-backed paper, install large rubber bands to the corners of the engraved surface, and then wrap the ceramic surface with a layer of corrugated stock. The foam-backed paper and corrugated stock provide protection from contamination and limited impact resistance. The rubber bands protect the sharp corners of the engraved surface protection from impact.

When securely wrapped, the anilox roll is placed in its shipping container, which could be new or used. If a used container is being employed, it will have been thoroughly inspected to ensure a safe delivery to the printer. Any damaged parts are replaced; or, if necessary, a new container is constructed.

For anilox rolls designed with a conventional journal configuration, the engraved surface is isolated from the inside of the shipping container by mounting the anilox roll on saddles that are secured to the container. When the rolls are secured by the journals, damage to the engraved surface is guaranteed, short of destruction of the entire container. Anilox rolls in sleeve and bored-journal configurations are secured in a similar manner to ensure a secure delivery.

About the Author...
Dan Foy is technical product specialist for HarperScientific. He conducts Walking Seminars™ for Harper, during which each of the 11 operations of the anilox roll manufacturing process is discussed in detail followed by a technical presentation of application and maintenance topics. He has been in the flexographic industry for 11 years.

CERAMIC ANILOX

CONVERSION FROM CHROME ROLLS
REAPS PRESSROOM BENEFITS

By Bill Poulson
& Todd Luman

At one time, using mechanically-engraved chrome anilox rolls was the only option that a converter had. These were operated with a rubber roll or a doctor-bladed metering system. Now, with the improved technology in the industry today, converting to ceramic anilox

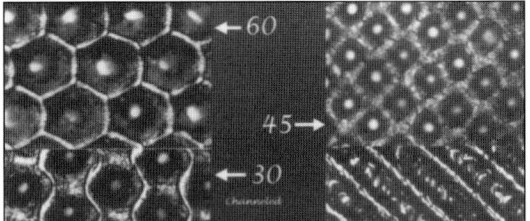

A laser-engraved ceramic anilox roll.

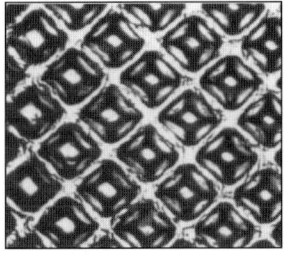

A chrome anilox roll.

rollers is a reality that many converters have experienced—and one that those who haven't experienced should consider.

Our intention in this article is to show the advantages of converting to ceramic anilox rolls by presenting the results of three trial press runs. We will also show improvements in deposit efficiencies when converting to a ceramic anilox roll.

Chrome-Engraved Aniloxes

Chrome anilox rolls are the original anilox technology. They are constructed of a steel base that is electroplated with copper and chrome. The roll surface is milled or engraved with a variety of tooling. Some chrome rolls are engraved using a diamond stylus. Any engraving method used on chrome rolls yields the same surface and wear characteristics.

Advantages of chrome rolls are:
- Good ink release.

- Good cell definition.

- Easy to clean.

Disadvantages of chrome anilox rolls are:
- Rapid wear; coat weights drop off quickly.

- Inefficient ink release.

- Wide cell walls.

A mechanically engraved anilox roll.

- Limited line screen selection.

- Limited geometry selection.

- Easily damaged.

- Environmentally hazardous to produce.

- Limitations in reproducibility.

- Susceptible to corrosion.

Laser Ceramic

A ceramic anilox roll is constructed of the same base steel as a chrome anilox roll. It is then built up with steel, and a chrome oxide ceramic powder is sprayed onto the roll. The chrome oxide is polished to a mirror finish, and then it is laser-engraved.

The buildup on a ceramic roll can be an arc-welded buildup, a spray buildup or HVOF buildup. Spray buildups are primarily used for sleeve technology.

HVOF is an excellent alternative to a corrosion barrier. The buildup materials can be various grades of steel.

Advantages of ceramic anilox rolls are:

• Excellent wear characteristics.

• Increased deposit efficiency.

• Better consistency of coat weight over time.

• Thin cell walls.

• Minimal post areas.

• Precision cell shapes.

• Higher line screens.

• Increased press speeds.

• Saturation specifications at lower coat weight.

• Spot engravings.

Disadvantages of ceramic-surfaced rolls are:

• Care is needed in cleaning of roll.

• Higher initial investment than chrome.

• Increase in reconditioning time (as compared to chrome).

Specifying Ceramic Roll

Inks and Specialty Coatings. In most cases, the ceramic roll will convert from chrome at a lower ink volume. There are many ink- and coating-related variables to be considered before an anilox can be specified. Coat weight, percentage of solids, viscosity and pound per gallon are critical specifications that need to be known.

You need to take into consideration the type of ink and whether the ink or coating is a solvent, water-born, EB, UV or other specialty coating type (adhesives, for example, would be considered a specialty type of coating). Metallic inks have larger particle sizes than standard inks. This also needs to be considered before specifying line screen.

Volume. Volume is the critical factor when specifying a ceramic anilox roll. Too often we get caught up in what line screen is needed, and we overlook volume. Know the cell dimensions of the engraving you are specifying. Every anilox manufacturer has its own line

screen and volume recommendations charted and published.

Line Screen. Once a volume is chosen for your application, it should then be placed within a line screen that fits the volume needed. Consider the particle size of pigments when specifying line screen. Ceramic does not yield the same surface tension as chrome and requires cell configurations to have efficient internal cell cavities.

When heavy-viscosity coatings are being applied, a shallow, free-flowing cell configuration is the appropriate cell profile. Thinner, less viscous coatings, on the other hand, should have an enclosed cell configuration to prevent the material from slinging. This may vary, depending on the chemistry of inks and coatings being used. Banded roll testing and experience will help determine the cell profile.

Banded Roll Testing

The key to a smooth transition in converting from mechanically-engraved chrome rolls to laser-engraved ceramic rolls is banded roll testing. A banded roll is a single anilox with various line screens, cell geometries and cell volumes. Banded rolls are primarily used in flexographic process printing to determine what line screen and volume will provide the optimal print densities, dot gain and print contrast for a given application. Although this is the most common type of testing conducted with banded rolls, testing is not necessarily limited

1st Press Run

Color	Coat Weight (Chrome Roll) 175l/s 10.5bcm	Coat Weight (Ceramic Roll) 145l/s 10.5bcm
Dark Beige	2.2gsm	3.2gsm
Neutral Beige	2.0gsm	3.2gsm
Red – Beige	2.2gsm	3.5gsm

2nd Press Run

Color	Coat Weight (Chrome Roll) 175l/s 10.5bcm	Coat Weight (Ceramic Roll) 180l/s 7.5bcm
Dark Beige	2.2gsm	2.1gsm
Neutral Beige	2.0gsm	2.1gsm
Red – Beige	2.2gsm	2.1gsm

3rd Press Run

Color	Coat Weight (Chrome Roll) 80l/s 17.2bcm	Coat Weight (Ceramic Roll) 140l/s 10.0bcm
Light Beige	2.0gsm	0.8gsm

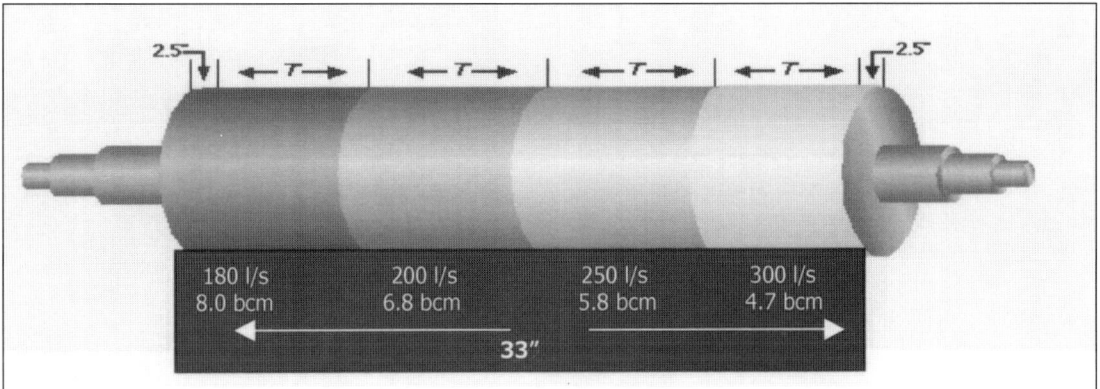

180 l/s
8.0 bcm

200 l/s
6.8 bcm

250 l/s
5.8 bcm

300 l/s
4.7 bcm

2.5

2.5

33"

The line screens and volumes as well as geometry of a banded roll will vary depending on what type of coating or ink is being used.

to that. Testing limits are determined by the time and dedication of the testers.

In order to have a successful trial, the personnel who will be involved in the test run—including management, prepress, co-suppliers and the person running the press—should define trial goals. Once the objectives are met and it is time for the press trial, the focus should be on making the banded roll perform the way it was designed, not on making the numbers fall into place by manipulation. A properly designed banded roll should have failing results as well as passing results, in order to see where the limitations are.

This approach was taken before the press trials described below were run. Much of the testing was with different ink formulas and substrates. The line screens and volumes, as well as the geometry, will vary depending on what type of coating or ink is being used. Banded roll testing is a well-thought-out way to determine the most efficient way to lay down your ink or coating.

Chrome to Ceramic

A series of press trials was performed to show efficiency of deposit rates of ceramic anilox rolls. A chrome anilox roll and an anilox that had been converted from chrome to ceramic were used. Our goal for this application was twofold: first, to match the performance of the chrome roll with that of the ceramic roll; and second, simply to provide an anilox with a longer life span.

The transfer efficiency of chrome engravings is usually much greater than that of ceramic engravings due to the smoothness of the chrome vs. the porosity of the ceramic. With this in mind, first a banded roll with various cell geometries and cell angles was designed.

The application that was converted used a 175-line screen chrome roll with a volume of 10.5. The target coat weight was 2.1gsm on paper. The recommended ceramic anilox roll was 145-line screen with a 10.5 volume. This beige, water-based ink had a pH of 8.9. The

viscosity was at 17 seconds on a #4 din cup. The initial job ran on the chrome roll.

In the first pressrun, the performance of the ceramic engravings surpassed all expectations and delivered many positive results. The most astonishing discovery was how efficient the ceramic roll was in transferring the coating. This allowed for increased press speeds, with noticeable improvement in print smoothness. The goal was to match a coat weight of 2.1gsm delivered by the chrome roll. The results achieved by the ceramic roll exceeded all expectations on all three shades of beige.

Another eye-opener was that when the test results were measured, not only did we have an improvement in press speeds and print quality, but we also achieved the same opacity, even though 1.2 gsm less ink was applied. This represented a reduction in ink usage of about 20 percent.

The increased deposit efficiency of the ceramic roll allowed for a reduction in cell volume and justification for more testing to be conducted. For the second pressrun, the new specification for the anilox was 180 L/S with a 7.5 volume. This was a 39 percent reduction in cell volume. Our goals remained the same: to achieve 2.1gsm. All other variables were constant with the exception of the running conditions. The new comparisons were to be done in a live production environment.

At the end of the second pressrun, the chrome roll was switched out and the ceramic roll was installed. Samples were taken and coat weight and spectro readings were done. The coat weight matched the chrome cylinder exactly at 2.1 gsm.

Third Press Trial

Because the results had been nothing but positive, a third press trial was run. The chrome roll was an 80-line screen 17.2bcm. The ceramic roll, in comparison, was a 140-line screen at a 10.0bcm. The coat weight using the chrome anilox was

2.0gsm and the coat weight with the ceramic roll was 0.8gsm. The goal of this trial was to reduce coat weight but still meet the color and opacity requirements.

Amazingly, the color and opacity requirements were achieved with a 1.2gms reduction in coat weight. In addition, the press speeds were increased from 150mpm (meters per minute) to 210mpm due to a thinner ink film being applied. This equated to a 40 percent reduction in ink usage and 40 percent increase in press efficiency. You can see the importance of making this conversion from chrome to ceramic anilox.

The improved performance of the ceramic roll over the chrome roll allowed for an increase of press speeds by as much as 70mpm. In the past, increasing press speed on the chrome roll lowered coat weight to unacceptable levels. This was not the case with the ceramic engravings. Press speeds increased and coat weight remained stable. Another notable improvement worth mentioning was the visual smoothness of the coating, which allowed us to reformulate the ink with less opaque white. This represents another cost saving that we were not expecting.

The colors tested were placed under three other colors. The other colors showed improvement of laydown because the base coat was improved. The conclusion drawn from the trial is that the higher cost of a ceramic roll over a chrome roll is justified not only by improvement in ink laydown, but also by significant savings in press time and ink cost. A cost saving was also achieved in reduced time matching ink at press.

Summary

Many advantages of ceramic anilox rolls have become evident through this conversion. All of the improvements are cost-effective and will be noticed in the reduced downtime and increased throughput on press. Advantages are:

- Increased stability of coat weight over the roll's life.

- Increased ink deposit efficiency.

- Ceramic geometries have thinner cell walls, allowing more area for ink and coatings.

The transfer efficiency of chrome engravings is usually much greater than that of ceramic engravings due to the smoothness of the chrome vs. the porosity of the ceramic.

- Improved laydown at lower volumes.

- Higher opacity on substrate.

- More controlled transfer of ink.

- The ceramic roll was manufactured with an efficient internal cell cavity.

- The coat weight remains the same at higher speeds; there is no drop-off, as occurred with the chrome roll. This resulted in ink savings of 35 cents to 51 cents per pound of paper, due to the 39 percent reduction in cell volume.

- Increased life span.

- Increased run time on press.

Conclusion

This conversion from chrome to ceramic has yielded many cost savings to the converter. If you are running graphic images, you will see a great improvement in print quality with the use of a ceramic anilox roll. In the printing applications described above, a paper substrate was used. Ceramic rolls can print on any substrate that will attract inks or coatings, including films, styrenes, wovens and tissue. Ceramic has a more controlled deposit rate, which will allow for an increase in quality over time.

About the Authors...
Bill Poulson is Northeast graphic consultant/Harper Graphic Solutions for Harper Corp. of America, Charlotte, NC. Todd Luman is customer product advocate for Harper.

Dimensional Tolerance

It May Be the "Missing Link" in Your Anilox Performance

By Art Ehrenberg

Most articles and technical presentations on anilox rolls seem to fall into four categories:

- Engraving (geometry, line screen, depth-to-opening ratios, etc.);

- Lasers (pulsed CO2, constant wave CO2, YAG);

- Ceramic coatings;

- Cleaning, care and maintenance.

All of these issues are very important and need to be studied and understood to develop a system around this component that will result in consistent printing. However, there is much more to anilox rolls that printers and anilox suppliers need to be concerned with in order for these critical components to perform correctly. The subject is dimensional tolerances.

We will look at some basic aspects of anilox roll dimension tolerances: bearings, bearing surfaces, gears

gear step diameters, key ways, balancing, TIR, cylindricity, circularity (roundness), engraved surface diameters etc. all must fall into certain tolerances in order for the rolls to perform properly. Often these subjects are taken too lightly, or the effects of these areas being out of tolerance are not fully understood. Let's take a look at some of these dimensions and tolerances.

Bearings and Bearing Surfaces

Bearing surface diameter sizes need to be within the tolerance that is specified by the bearing manufacturer. These specifications can vary depending on the type of bearings used and the fit required. Different bearings have different tolerances in respect to the bore size (I.D.), the outer diameter (O.D), the allowable run-out, the load rating, etc. The run-out tolerance for a bearing is the allowance given for the bearing's inner race to run out of round or in an eccentric condition from its absolute center axis. This tolerance may be described in various ways, and we will address "run out" and "roundness" a little later.

Today there are a number of printers who do not have blueprints for their presses and do not know what the bearing surface outer diameter tolerance or run-out allowance of their rollers should be. Yes, one would assume this not to be true, but it is. The easiest way to find out is to call the press manufacturer. Another way to find a bearing surface size is to locate the bearing manufacturer's name, which is usually stamped on the bearing housing along with the bearing number. Then

Shaft Tolerances	
1/2" – 1-15/16"	Plus .0000" to minus .0005"
2" – 3"	Plus .0000" to minus .0010"
3-3/16" – Up	Plus .0000" to minus .0015"

Bearing Bore Tolerances	
1/2" – 5/8"	Plus .0008" to minus .0000"
3/4" – 1-15/16"	Plus .0009" to minus .0000"
2" – 3"	Plus .0010" to minus .0000"
3 – 3/16" Up	Plus .0012" to minus .0000"

and balancing. Total indicated runout (TIR), circularity, concentricity and cylindricity will be discussed, as well as how these aspects of anilox roll dimensioning are often confused.

No matter what cell geometry, line screen or depth-to-opening you're using, what type of laser was utilized to perform the engraving, what level of quality the ceramic is or how well you clean and maintain your rolls, these rolls will not perform without proper dimensional stability.

Components such as bearing surfaces diameters,

call a bearing supplier to get the specifications. The table below is an example of the diameter tolerances for a particular brand of a flange-mounted bearing. With this information, you can determine the required tolerance of the size for the bearing to fit properly.

As an example, by using this table for this particular bearing, you can see that if you have a bearing with a bore size of 1/2 inch (.500 inch), then one possible tolerance for the bearing surface, called here the "shaft tolerance," would be .500-inch maximum diameter to .4995-inch minimum diameter. (The shafts on the ends of anilox rolls are also sometimes referred to as "journals.")

As an anilox supplier, I have seen countless complications while trying to help customers with tolerance issues. Some rolls we see for reconditioning are from older or modified presses or acquired used presses, and no blueprints for the anilox are available. Since we as the anilox supplier are responsible for the performance of the entire roll, we have to know the size for verification. The response by many customers is, "Don't worry about repairing them, they looked good when we took the rolls out." Other customers get a little upset when we have to tell them the bearing surfaces need repair for being undersized, and that there will be additional charges for that service. Some customers won't pay the additional charges, and say "Let them go." Later, they wonder why they are going through bearings so quickly, or why they are having printing complications.

Undersized bearing surfaces can cause roll chatter and alignment problems, and they may reduce the life of the bearing and destroy the bearing surface on the shaft. Poorly maintained bearings can freeze up during operation, causing severe damage to shafts, sometimes to the point of requiring total replacement of shaft steps.

Maintenance crews or anyone removing old bearings and installing new ones should take care that no excessive damage is done to the bearing surface or the bearing itself. We see hundreds of rolls per year that have gouges, nicks and dings on critical shaft dimensions or roll face edges caused by hammers, screw drivers, bar stocks and any imaginable tool that could be used to beat a bearing off a shaft.

A general rule of thumb is: DO NOT BEAT BEARINGS ON AND OFF SHAFTS. Mishandling during installation of bearings can also cause bent shafts, which can cause excessive TIR that can lead to printing problems and reduced bearing life. TIR, in respect to the anilox roll, is the comparison of how well the roller body (engraved area) runs concentric to the bearing surfaces on the roll shafts. Generally speaking, a bearing shaft should have a TIR of no more than .0005-inch.

Invest in a good bearing puller for the removal of bearings, and follow bearing manufacturer instructions for installing them. A bearing warmer can be used to expand the bearing race slightly before installation for more of a shrink fit, or to simply aid in the installation.

No matter what cell geometry, line screen or depth-to-opening you're using, what type of laser was utilized to perform the engraving, what level of quality the ceramic is or how well you clean and maintain your anilox rolls, they will not perform without proper dimensional stability. (Photo courtesy of The Harper Corp.)

When you are installing internal bearings, put the bearing in a freezer for an hour or so to shrink the bearing so it drops into the bore, then seals as it comes to ambient temperature. In addition, take care that the bearing shaft surface is free of rough spots and burrs. Also make sure the bore of the bearing for O.D. fits – or the O.D of the bearing for I.D. fits – is clean. It is also a good idea to apply a very thin oil film to the matting surfaces before installation. A slight radius on the bearing surface step or chamber on a bearing bore will also make the installation easier. If you improperly install a bearing, it can be damaged or can remove surface area from the bearing surface or bore surface. The result is that these surfaces will be out of round or improperly sized, which will affect future fits and possibly lead to TIR problems. This can affect print quality and add unnecessary costs to the reconditioning of your rolls.

Most "standard inch" bearings used for printing applications will be installed to an RC, or "running and sliding," fit. This fit does not require pressing or other means of excessive force for the bearing to be installed. It is typically used for high-precision fits, gauges, high-friction machinery and most all other moving parts.

Gears

Gears on the anilox roller shafts follow the same handling, mounting and removal rules as bearings. As with bearings, when gears do not fit properly, "chatter" or harmonic vibrations may result, which can damage shafts, keyways and gears.

When a keyway becomes excessively worn, it is usually perfectly acceptable (from a performance standpoint) to mill a new keyway 180 degrees from the old one in the same shaft. One crucial area to focus on when milling new keyways is centering: It must be exactly centered on the shaft. If not, the key will not fit. Proper length and width of the keyway is important for a snug fit, as is the use of proper mills for the correct keyway shape. Verification of keyway width should be done by gauge blocks and not dial calipers.

Another troublesome issue with gear steps is a lack of attention to the steps TIR. Severe TIR on any step of an anilox shaft can be a problem. This can lead to "gear chatter" caused by gears bottoming out or uneven matting of gears, which, if severe enough, can result in the chatter effect transferring a pattern to the printed substrate. This condition will also wear gears prematurely. As with bearing removal and installation, we see many rolls that were damaged during the installation and/or removal of gears.

Mishandling is usually evident by excessive scratches and gouges on the gear steps and possibly on neighboring steps (when the hammer slips). Scratches and dings on shaft steps may just be cosmetic issues and may not necessarily require extensive repair. They may just cause difficulty in removal or installation, and may simply require a filing to remove burrs or displaced metal. Where the anilox supplier has issues is when the damages, which may only be superficial, interfere with obtaining measurements for specification verification.

Gear steps can have a TIR of around .005-inch without affecting the performance of the roll, but this will vary depending on the press manufacturer and gear tolerances. Some OEMs have very tight tolerances on these steps due to designs that are vulnerable to shafts flexing. In this way, the tolerance will allow for some flexing without hindering the performance of the roller. All anilox suppliers should be checking for bent shafts and damages on all roll shaft steps during the initial and final inspection stages of the process, and should be documenting them. Particularly on the initial inspection of used rolls, alerting customers to bent and damaged journals will help them address the problem internally, which will hopefully result in modifying practices and procedures to reduce the damages and subsequent cost of repairs.

In most cases, the person ordering the anilox is not the person installing or removing it, so communication of these issues needs to be clear among all parties. Often, poor communication leads to finger-pointing sessions. This is all the more reason why good documentation/communication on the part of the anilox supplier and the customer is so important.

One way of measuring TIR is by resting the roll's bearing surfaces in a slot made by placing two precision bearings closely together in a housing.

Balancing Procedures

Balancing of anilox rolls can be a critical factor, depending on the press tolerances and the nature and quality of the printing required. There are two types of balancing procedures: static and dynamic. An analogy is the balancing of car tires. The old bubble balancing is the static procedure; spin balancing is the dynamic procedure.

An unbalanced roll can lead to harmonic vibration at different speeds, just as with a car tire, and can cause all sorts of problems on press. Anilox suppliers should be checking for this condition during the initial inspection stages of anilox reconditioning, and should report the findings to the customer. It is quite common (particularly on larger rolls, such as for corrugated) to see balancing weights welded on the inside of the tubing when the roll was manufactured. In some cases, the weights break loose, which will result in an unbalanced condition. In most cases, you can hear the weight rattling around inside the tube, alerting you to the condition.

Sometimes loose weights can get caught up in and be muffled by other debris left inside the tube during manufacturing. The more appropriate balancing technique would be to drill out amounts of material at each end of the finished roll face and either leave them empty to reduce weight in that area or insert a rod stock of steel to add weight if needed. Then tack-weld the rod in place. If the raw tube is too far out of balance, however, welded-in weights may have to be used. Proper dynamic balancing is usually done to a specific roll RPM or FPM (surface feet per minute).

Balancing is usually not required on narrow-web rolls. This is due to the fact that many are manufactured from solid stock rather than from tubes. The size of the roll, the construction practices and the nature of the running dynamics of most narrow-web presses are different from presses with larger rolls.

When manufacturing new anilox roll bases for any wide web or corrugated press, top-quality tubing should be utilized to reduce the amount of mechanical balancing required.

As anilox suppliers, we have the ability to use any grade tubing to build a new roll if it is not specified on a blueprint from the press manufacturer. I prefer to see a "hot rolled seamless" tubing of a very high grade, which, among other things, will guarantee that the tubing wall thickness is uniform to a tighter specification, and in turn reduces the need for excessive balancing.

As with most everything in life, you get what you pay for, and high-grade tubing comes with a price. Pricing in high-grade tubing vs. low-grade can be significant. Your anilox supplier should have a specifica-

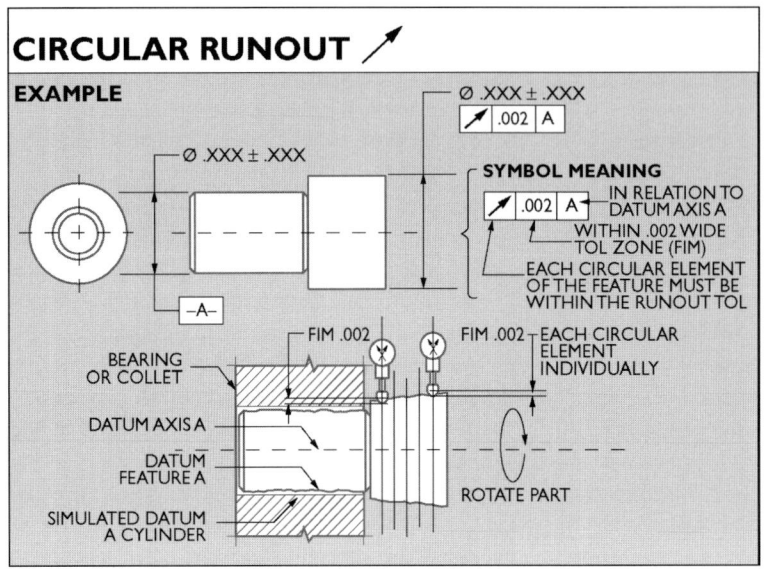

Figure 1

concerned with the TIR between the bearing surfaces and the engraved body. This is where lack of dimensional stability typically has the most effect on the roll's ability to evenly apply a liquid film and pressure to the printing plate. A TIR measurement between the bearing surfaces and the engraving is taken to ensure that the roll does not rotate in an egg shaped or eccentric condition from its axis when mounted during anilox processing or in the press. TIR that is out of tolerance can cause cylinder bounce, harmonic vibrations and uneven impression of the anilox to the plate, which can result in dot gain in areas and / or light and dark printing streaks.

TIR is usually measured in one of two ways. In most instances, the roll's bearing surfaces are rested in a slot made by placing two precision bearings closely together in a housing (see photo), or in a set of metal blocks with a "V" cut out of them. These set-ups are called "bearing blocks" or "V" blocks, respectively. After mounting in the blocks, a precision dial indicator is used to measure the TIR on the circumference of the roll.

With this method of TIR measurement, "circularity" or "roundness" of the bearing surface must be taken into consideration. Out-of-round conditions, flat spots or burrs from scratches and dings on the bearing shaft surface could exaggerate or even cancel out the true TIR reading. This is due to the fact that there are two

tion for a high-grade tubing for all new anilox rolls.

Understanding your anilox rolls' dimensional specifications and how they relate to your press, its print performance and anilox maintenance is key in reducing downtime, saving money and maintaining high quality.

Cleaning, care and maintenance of anilox rolls are very important, as are the engraving, lasers and ceramic coatings. No matter what cell geometry, line screen or depth-to-opening you're using, however, or what type of laser was utilized to perform the engraving, or what level of quality the ceramic is or how well you clean and maintain your rolls, these rolls will not perform without proper dimensional stability.

Total Indicated Runout (TIR)

Total indicated runout describes how certain features of a part run true to the absolute axis of the part. The term "TIR" utilized in the anilox arena typically is a numerical expression of how the bearing surfaces on the shafts of a roller run round or concentric to each other and the engraved area of the roll body when rotated. The term is often confused with "circularity" and "concentricity."

The term "circular runout" defines the circular condition of a single step or plane of a single-part feature to a datum axis (see *Figure 1*). The difference between "circular" and "total runout" is described in *Figure 2*. The engraver is most

Figure 2

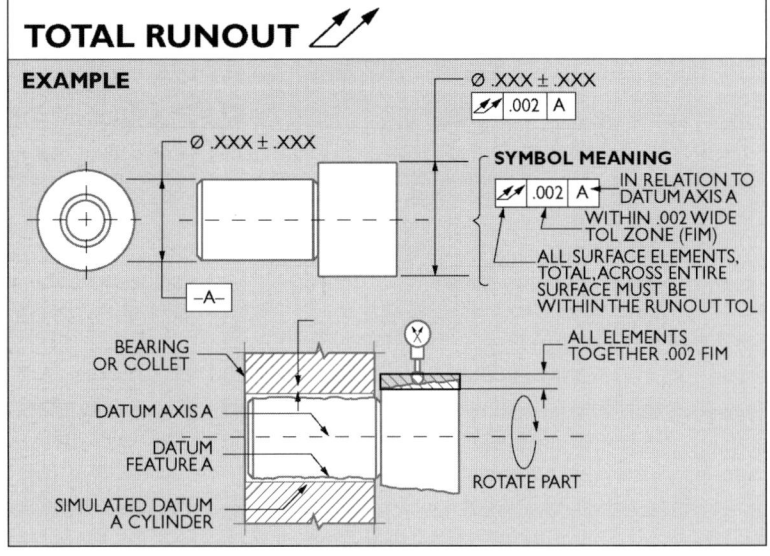

areas of the bearing surface touching two surfaces of the bearings or "V" blocks simultaneously. If you are using bearing blocks, check the bearings periodically for accuracy, and replace when necessary. Bearing and "V" blocks also should be on a level surface when performing TIR checks.

Another method of measuring TIR is to hold and rotate the roll between two centers in a lathe-like fixture or in a conventional lathe between a chuck and a center. This set-up will give the truest reading of TIR between the bearing surfaces and the engraved body, because you no longer have the influence of the bearings in the bearing blocks. Check the circularity of the steps. After the roll is set in one of the described methods, a dial indicator is put against the roll body and the roll rotated to obtain the variance reading of how much the roll body runs in and away from the center axis of the roll.

It is a good idea for converters to be capable of checking TIR in and out of their presses. If you choose to purchase and use a dial indicator, purchase a high-quality brand and make certain not to introduce it to impact. They are sensitive instruments and must be maintained properly in order to give correct readings. Also be certain to acquire a high-quality, rigid base for holding the indicator.

The measurement of TIR on rolls with internal bearings is much the same, but must be performed on a precision shaft either from the OEM or one manufactured to OEM tolerances. With these rolls, there should be no locking device holding the roll to the shaft, which applies undue pressure to the core. This can seat the roll in an undesirable position because of the bearing tolerance. The shaft ends should be running true to the bearing surface areas of the shafts to no more than .0002-inch as a reference point. Place a dial indicator at 90 degrees to the roll axis pointing directly downward over the center of the roll.

The TIR tolerance that is specified for the press you have is different from the TIR that is acceptable during the anilox manufacturing process. Take a wide web roll, for example, that has a TIR tolerance of .0015-inch.

Generally acceptable TIR tolerances for the engraved body to the bearing surfaces:

Corrugated	.0015" to .0025"
Preprint	.001" to .0015"
Film, Foil, Other Wide Web	.0005" to .0015"
Tag, Label, Envelope	.0005" to .001"

Let's assume that a roll is circularly round but has a slightly bent shaft, causing a TIR of .001-inch on the engraved area prior to engraving. If the TIR cannot be eliminated by manipulation of the laser's chuck and tailstock devices, a portion of the roll surface will be moving into and away from the laser beam as much as .001-inch. If the engraving is going to be a 400 L/S at a 3.3 BCM, the engraving depth will be about 13 microns, or roughly .0005-inch. If the roll body is moving into and away from the laser beam by .001-inch, one side of the roll's engraving will be far too deep and the other far too shallow. This results in thick and thin ink films on different planes of the engraving, which will cause light and dark printing across the web. So, the roll's TIR tolerance to run in the press is not necessarily acceptable to use during anilox processing.

Circularity (Roundness)

Along with TIR, we must also consider the roundness of the roll body or the engraved diameter in particular. This can be a tricky subject, and the associated terminology often varies or is misapplied.

Circularity is described in the dictionary a couple of different ways, depending on the dictionary you use. Two of those descriptions are "the quality or state of being circular" and "the roundness of a two-dimensional figure." Circularity is a tolerance zone formed between two concentric circles where the surface periphery at any cross section perpendicular to the axis must fall within the specified tolerance. An example of a specific tolerance can be seen in *Figure 3*.

Cylindricity applies to the entire cylinder length, not just one area (see *Figure 4*). Circularity and cylindricity have to be considered with concentricity in order to get a better picture of the roll's dimensional stability. These geometric measurements will also affect the roll's ability to engrave evenly around the circumference.

In the machining and/or grinding stages of anilox production, very special care must be taken to address TIR, circularity, cylindricity and concentricity in order for the roller to meet high quality standards. In manual machining or lathing, it is possible for a roller to not be circular and for this condition to not be revealed by the use of a dial indicator alone. This usually occurs when machine components such as head stock bearings and centers contain run-out that is out of tolerance. Therefore, a couple of measuring methods must be applied to be certain you are within the allowable tolerances of each of these conditions.

When dealing with tolerances, consider all the components' tolerances that will affect the overall performance of the anilox roll. The anilox bearing surface has a specific size and "runout" tolerance, but so does the bearing. Therefore, make certain that both components are all in tolerance in order to achieve the expected results.

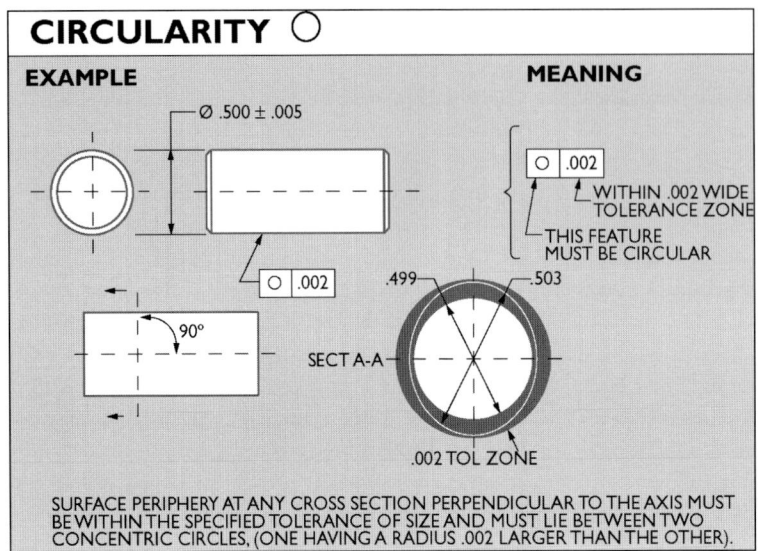

Figure 3

The stability of all the dimensional tolerances of anilox rolls is important. Often many of these dimensions are neglected, especially during bearing and gear removal, and the effects of their being out of tolerance are not always understood. The anilox roll supplier is responsible for the roll's overall performance, so it must have all the tolerances to the correct specifications; otherwise, the roll's performance will be compromised no matter how precise the engraving was performed.

As flexographic printing continues in an upward spiral to new quality heights, these dimensional tolerances are getting tighter and tighter. We must understand the dynamics of the tolerances, have the equipment and technique to measure them and hold them to their acceptable limits. Printers must understand how the handling of these rolls can affect the tolerances and how out-of-specification tolerances can affect the printing requirements.

You must stack tolerances to get the true picture of the total dimensional stability. Take a roll that runs on internal bearings, for example. This type of roll will be fit to a shaft and will either use the bearings for the rotation of the roll or use them simply for insertion of the shaft that drives the roll. With this set-up, multiple components must be in tolerance. All the tolerances must be realistically combined to get the total "stack tolerance."

With an internal bearing arrangement, you have the size tolerance of the roll's bore (I.D., or inner diameter) that the bearing goes into, plus its allowable circular tolerance. You have the tolerance of the run-out in the bearing itself and the bearing inner-race bore diameter plus the tolerance of the bearing surface diameter on the shaft that is inserted through the bearing bore. Then you have to consider the run-out tolerance of the shaft as it is mounted in the press.

In order to get the true picture of the maximum allowable run-out condition of the engraved portion of the anilox roll, consider all these tolerances and how they may add or "stack" together. So if the roll bearing is allowed to run-out .0005-inch, and the shaft .0005-inch, and the bore of the roll .0005-inch, and when the diameter tolerance of the shaft and the bore tolerance of the bearing inner race and the bore tolerance of the roll body are considered, there could realistically be a run-out or TIR of .0015-inch or more.

About the author...
Art Ehrenberg is vice president of operations for Harper Corporation's Green Bay, WI division. He has held numerous titles within Harper's organization, including plant manager at the company's Charlotte, N.C., headquarters from 1990 to 1996. He has been associated with the flexographic printing industry for 21 years.

Note: The drawings in this article were reprinted from "A Pocket Guide To Geo-Metrics II," pp. 12, 13, 18, 19, 17, with the permission of Pearson Edwards Inc., Upper Saddle River, NJ.

Figure 4

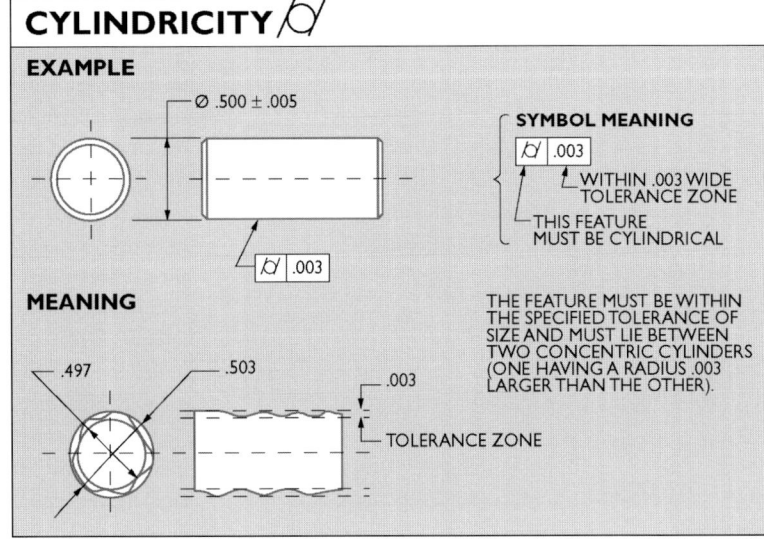

IMPLEMENTING AN ANILOX PROTECTION PROGRAM

PRESS AND PRESSROOM COMPONENTS MAKE THE DIFFERENCE BETWEEN SUCCESS AND FAILURE

By Bobby Furr

Over the past several years, the chrome anilox roll has been nearly phased out and the laser-engraved ceramic anilox has become the anilox roll of choice. With the end user requiring more and more detail in the graphics, the anilox line screen has gone from 360 lines per inch to 550, 800, even as high as 2000 lines per inch.

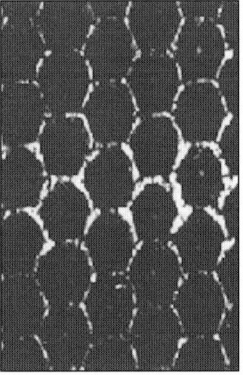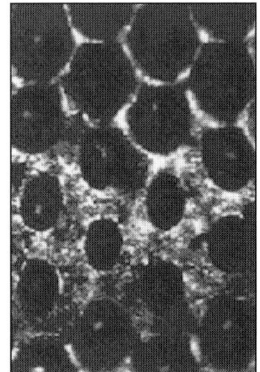

Anilox rolls that are severely plugged with ink (right) and damaged by a caustic cleaner (left).

While flexography can consistently match or provide even better print quality than offset and gravure, our investment is quite expensive. While some of us have played the stock market at one time or another, in some of these cases we have been skeptical on just how secure our investment was. Within the flexographic realm, we can – with the right program – protect our investment.

A typical press can cost in excess of $1 million dollars. Your ink investment can sometimes easily exceed hundreds of thousands of dollars. Depending on how many presses you have, the anilox investment can run into the hundreds of thousands of dollars, as well.

Protecting Your Investment

The press should be routinely maintained and cleaned on a weekly basis. Letting ink stay on the press, the gears, the hoses and the anilox can ultimately hinder your operation and can cause delays due to inadequate operation.

When a new anilox is received, a quality certification document should be kept on file with a photograph of the engraving and the correct line screen and volume as it was received. This is important because, should you have density problems on press, you can analyze the anilox roll as it is and reference back to when the roll

was purchased. If the anilox is clean and you have had a significant decrease in depth of the engraved cells, this could tell you that the engraving is worn and it is time to replace the anilox roll. If the engraved cells show visual dried ink pigment and clogging of ink or coating in the cells, then the roll is plugged and is probably the reason you are losing color on the press.

Protecting your anilox investment should be standard within your facility. First and foremost, all anilox rolls should be covered with protective roll covers. I can't tell you how many times I've seen a press operator – who obviously knows nothing about the delicate engraved cells and ceramic coating on an anilox roll – playing drums on the anilox roll with a wrench. Sound far-fetched? It's true; it happens all the time. That person has just damaged a very expensive anilox roll. With a minimal investment in protective roll covers, the return is huge.

Look at Press Conditions

To further ensure protection of your anilox roll, examine your press conditions. Believe it or not, the majority of reconditioned rolls are not worn out – they are damaged. The most common reasons why rolls are damaged in the press are improper blade pressure, inferior blade material and inadequate filtration of the inking system.

Doctor blade particles, improperly ground ink particles and ceramic particles are the most common cause of anilox score lines. These particles circulate through the ink train and lodge behind the doctor blade. A grinding effect from the particle occurs and causes shiny lines on the anilox roll.

Filtration and magnets within the inking system

Identifying Quality Of Steel

Doctor blade particles, improperly ground ink particles and ceramic particles are the most common cause of anilox score lines.

Anilox Roll Protection

This roll storage racking system is set up to be mobile and easily brought to the presses.

should be mandatory. Most printers will mount the filter canister – which includes an internal magnet – to the out-feed of the pump or somewhere within the in-feed line. The filter should be between 20- and 40-mesh screen size. The magnet should have a minimum pull rate of 2 lbs. for presses of 20 inches and smaller; and up to 8 lbs. for presses of more than 20 inches. The filters and magnets should be cleaned after each run. It takes about three minutes to clean the pictured filter and magnet. Some filter canisters are harder to get to and take longer to clean up.

High-Quality End-Seals

Another common problem is end-seal leaking. Something as small as an end seal can result in major problems and major dollar expenditure. A good analogy is buying a car. If you bought a new Cadillac and you had to pay extra for the tires, would you put used tires on it? You probably would buy a high-quality, name-brand tire that would last a long time.

We pay millions of dollars for the press; its parts should be of good quality. Most printers will try to save money on the material cost of the end-seal. In many cases, the end-seal will be of a foam material, which is the least expensive. This results in the end-seal leaking severely, so the operator cranks down on the chamber system or increases the air-loaded pressure. By doing this, he has already started prematurely wearing out his anilox roll, increasing the ink leakage and wearing out the seals even faster. For a couple of dollars, a good-quality end-seal could be the determining factor in protecting your anilox investment and saving thousands of dollars.

Cleaning and Maintenance

One of the most important steps to protect your anilox investment is cleaning and maintaining your anilox roll. A common question is, "How do you recommend that we clean our anilox rolls?"

Printers spend tens of thousands of dollars replacing anilox rolls that don't need to be replaced because they think that the engraved cells are worn out. Press operators sometimes neglect cleaning the anilox roll properly when they change colors because they don't have the right on-press cleaner, steel brush or automated wash-up solutions.

The reality is that chemical cleaners are in daily use in the flexo printing industry, and – for the most part – they work. Many of these cleaners are caustic to permit fast and thorough cleaning.

Protecting your anilox investment should be a science, not an art. Printers who have an anilox protection program in place estimate annual cost savings of tens of thousands of dollars.

A standard practice when using a chemical cleaner is to use a stainless steel brush to agitate the cleaner. The finest bristles on a brush are .003 diameter. The bristles can only reach the bottom of the cell in engravings of 280 line screen (cell opening of 85 microns = 3.34 thousandths) or less. This does not mean that because you have a 700-line screen anilox roll, you cannot use a stainless steel brush. On the contrary, it is good to agitate the surface of the ceramic as well as the tops of the cell walls to loosen the ink. A steel brush will not damage the anilox roll.

Precautions should be taken when choosing a specific cleaning solution. More times than not, an anilox roll is damaged because of the pH of the chemical solution. The normal pH of the cleaner for water-based ink is between 8.5 and 9.4 pH. Having a pH meter on hand is definitely a plus. In order to be effective, the pH of a chemical cleaner should always be higher than the pH of the ink. In most situations, corrosion is most likely to occur at a pH below 4 and above 11.8. Although extremely effective, anilox cleaners outside this range can damage engravings if exposure is prolonged.

The last step in protecting your anilox investment is storing your anilox rolls correctly. Anilox rolls should not be stored in boxes or crates. Too many times, the roll gets bumped while it is taken out or put into a box or crate. For a minor investment, roll storage racks can be obtained and mounted in the pressroom or, depending on the size of the anilox rolls, can be placed on roll storage racking systems and made to be easily maneuvered or actually rolled to the press.

To summarize, protecting your anilox investment should be a science, not an art. Printers who have an anilox protection program in place estimate annual cost savings of tens of thousands of dollars. An anilox protection program will minimize waste, minimize downtime, minimize anilox roll reconditioning and keep your investment protected. ▨

About the Author...
Bobby Furr is technical product manager for Harper Scientific, Charlotte, NC. He is an 18-year industry veteran who has worked on the manufacturing of anilox rolls and has served as a technical press consultant. He can be reached at www.harperscientific.com.

THE INVISIBLE ENEMY

ANILOX CLEANER pH EXTREMES CAN WREAK HAVOC ON YOUR ROLLS

By Elias Haddadin and Art Ruge

The production process of the graphic arts industry, like all manufacturing processes, is faced with the inevitable effects of time on its equipment. Regretfully, no press can continue to run indefinitely without preventative maintenance and actual repairs. Sooner or later, bearings need to be greased, or friction will cause them to seize up. If tracks aren't lubricated, machines cannot open and close. Furthermore, among other important tasks, one cannot ignore the heart of the press, the anilox roll, which must be re-engraved over time due to wear, otherwise the press will starve from lack of sufficient ink to produce good color strength.

These examples are familiar to most, especially to press operators and maintenance personnel. There is, however, an invisible enemy in many plants that can also cause harm to the anilox roll. This enemy very seldom produces visible damage immediately, but slowly over time. It usually takes months, if not longer, of repeated usage before it makes its presence felt. In time, it will cause the anilox roll to corrode, and possibly the ceramic coating to chip and eventually cause it to blister.

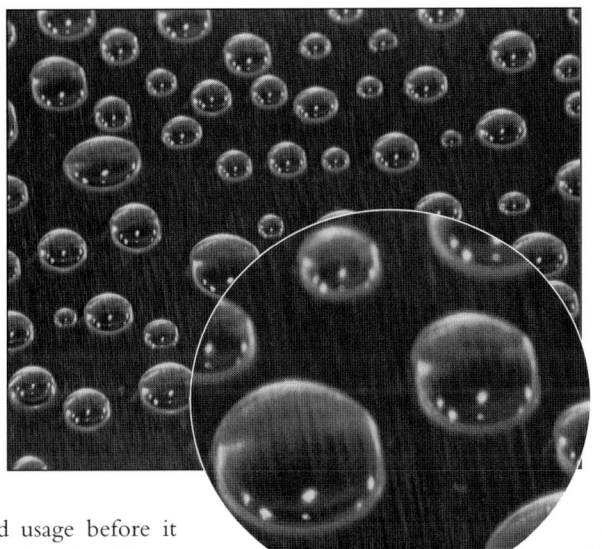

This invisible enemy is the pH level (alkalinity or acidity) of the cleaning solution that is used to clean anilox rolls. Although the same concept may apply to the ink in some extreme cases, this discussion will be limited to the cleaners only. Based on past observations, anilox roll corrosion problems can be minimized if the pH range is maintained anywhere between 6 and 10.5. This precautionary measure is based on the premise that the chances of developing undercoat corrosion condition increase as the pH approaches either extreme on the pH scale.

The Corrosion Process

Cleaning solutions that are near either extreme of the pH scale must first get underneath the ceramic coating of the anilox roll in order to cause any harm to the roll. The plasma-sprayed coating of chrome oxide ceramic, which is applied to all laser-engraved anilox rolls, has a small degree of porosity. This porosity allows liquids to eventually penetrate the coating and come into contact with the underlying base metals, mainly steel. Chrome-plated, mechanically engraved rolls are also susceptible to the corrosion process in a somewhat similar fashion.

Some anilox roll manufacturers use specially formulated organic coating as sealant on their laser-engraved rolls as a last pass to impede this process and, in some cases, improve transfer characteristics of the roll surface itself. In spite of taking these measures, however, most often continued and excessive use of cleaning methods – other than chemical cleaners such as soda blasting – can eventually break down the sealant. Once the underlying metals come into contact with those highly acidic or highly alkaline cleaning solutions, the corrosion process begins underneath the ceramic coating layer or under the chrome layer in the mechanically engraved rolls. Corrosion byproducts, such as oxides and hydroxides of iron, accumulate underneath the surface coating, causing a localized blister at that site.

Water Dilution

Some use a high pH cleaning solution, but dilute it with water. Wouldn't this reduce the pH to a safe level? The answer is absolutely "no." To comprehend just how powerful a cleaner with a pH at either extreme of the pH scale can be, it is important to understand how the pH scale works.

Because the pH scale represents the logarithm of

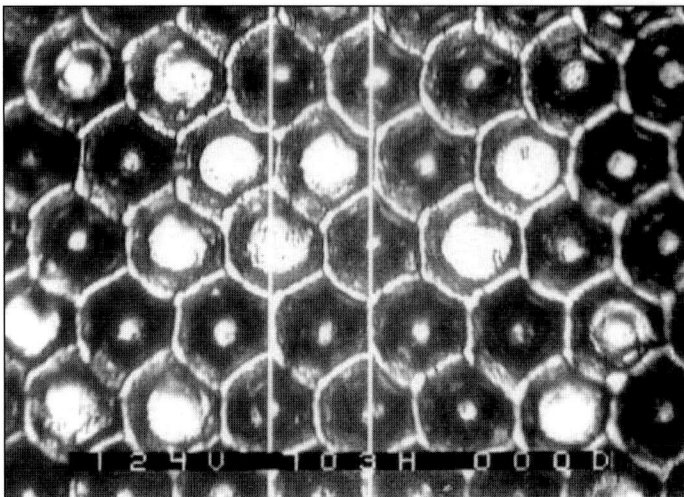

Figure 1. Photomicrograph of plugged cells and cleaned cells.

the inverse hydrogen ion concentration in a solution, the higher the hydrogen ion concentration, the lower the pH. This means a low pH for acidic solutions. By the same token, the lower the hydrogen ion concentration, the higher the pH and the more alkaline the solution.

Furthermore, because the pH scale is logarithmic, diluting the cleaning solution with water at a 1:1 ratio does not mean the pH level will be reduced at the same ratio. For example, the pH of a solution at pH 12.4 may be reduced by only a few tenths of a pH unit after it is diluted at 4:1 water-to-concentrate ratio. Similarly, an increase in pH from 9.0 to 10.0, for example, represents a tenfold increase in the alkalinity of that solution. Many cleaning solutions are sold in a concentrated form for reducing shipping cost, to be diluted later with water by the end user. It is vital, therefore, for the long-term survival of your anilox roll to know the final pH level of the diluted cleaner.

Anilox rolls that have been subjected to solutions with extremely high or low pH have always been vulnerable to corrosion. This problem has existed for years in such areas as the paper towel and tissue markets, where the inks are actually formulated with low pH to improve print quality. If inks or cleaners with pH levels at either extreme of the pH scale are to be used, it is highly advisable that the anilox roll supplier is consulted.

How the Problem Developed

Unfortunately, this problem of pH extremes is beginning to surface in the corrugated industry. Here's a quick look at how it developed. First, the ever-increasing demands for improved production and thus faster press speeds has forced ink companies to develop quicker-drying inks. These inks not only dry faster on the substrate, but also – with time and intermittent usage – can dry on the anilox roll, plugging the cells (see *Figure 1*).

Further compounding this problem is the use of higher line screens, which are necessary to produce point-of-purchase displays and other graphic work. These high-screen rolls are very difficult to clean when they are plugged. As line screen increases, the cell opening decreases and it becomes impossible for even the smallest bristles of a fine stainless steel brush to enter the cell because they are larger than the cell opening. The size of the bristle for a fine stainless steel brush is, on average, about 75 microns. Line screens higher than 330 LPI have cell openings smaller than 75 microns.

Second, faced with this new dilemma, the cleaning processes have changed significantly over the last few years. One of the first developments was an entire new group of "pressure" cleaners, not to mention ultrasonic cleaning. The pressure cleaning devices are designed to bombard the dry ink in the cells with tiny particles using machines equipped with a traversing mechanism to produce an even surface appearance. The use of the manual version is not recommended. The powdered materials are impinged on the surface of the anilox roll using compressed air at a relatively low pressure to blast away at the dried ink (10-12 psi has been used without causing visible deterioration to the roll surface).

While most of these cleaning methods can be effective in cleaning plugged cells, the basic process of abrasion that allows them to clean will also accelerate the loss of cell volume over time due to wear. If pressure-cleaning equipment is operated properly and used sparingly, however, it can enhance the cleaning process considerably, especially in stubborn cases when chemical cleaning fails to do the job. On the other hand, one must keep in mind that these methods of cleaning may not provide a solution to the problem; neither replaces everyday chemical cleaning.

In answer to this problem, the manufacturers of the anilox rolls recommend washing up anilox rolls as quickly as possible with a "good" cleaner. This advice has led to a variety of new products. Commercial cleaners that were never intended for use to clean anilox rolls have also been used. (Some plants were even using oven cleaners, not realizing they have a pH level over 13, which could cause severe harm to the anilox roll.) Many of these cleaning solutions were never checked for their pH level. Some were effective and some were not. But the consistent use of those cleaners over time, with pH at either

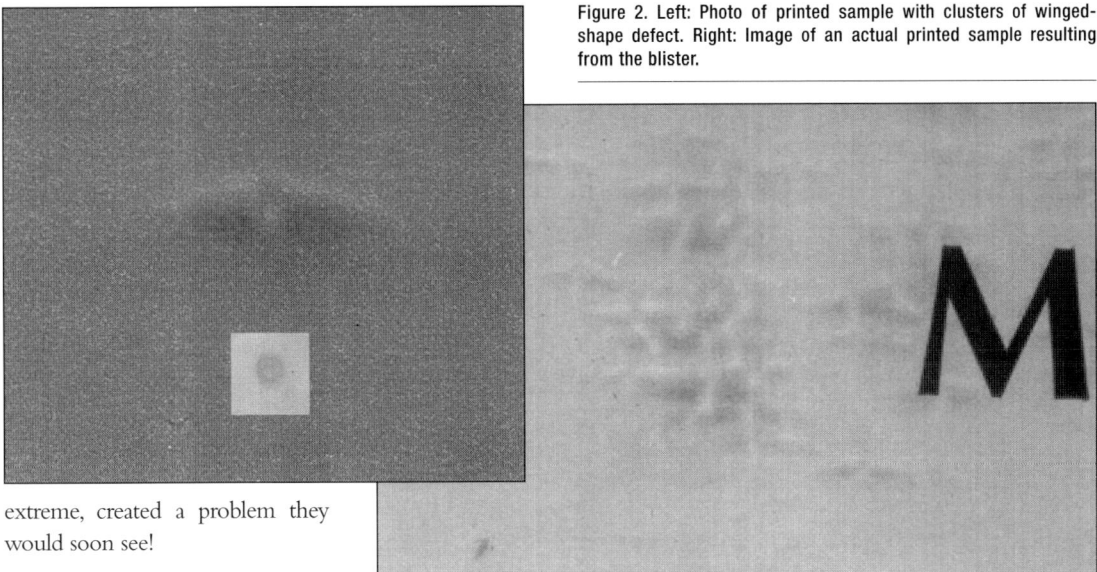

Figure 2. Left: Photo of printed sample with clusters of winged-shape defect. Right: Image of an actual printed sample resulting from the blister.

extreme, created a problem they would soon see!

No Longer Invisible

When blistering first begins on the anilox rolls, it is often difficult to detect on the roll itself. The first place it is usually noticed is on the printed substrate, especially in the large, solid block areas. In this example, the doctor blade meters the ink over the entire face of the roll, except when it comes into contact with the raised area caused by the blister. This raised area loses its cell-carrying capacity very rapidly due to the high abrasive force created by the doctor blade.

Consequently, very little or no ink will transfer to the printing plate, resulting in a relatively lighter print on the substrate. The raised area, on the other hand, will cause relatively more ink to accumulate on either side of the blister, resulting in a relatively darker print on both sides of the blister. In the microphotographs in *Figure 2*, the photo at left shows cells at the blister, indicating heavy wear, and cells away from the site of the blister. The right photo shows an actual winged pattern in a printed sample resulting from a blistered anilox roll. This winged pattern can help locate the blisters on the surface of the anilox roll.

Once the blistering problem becomes visible in the printed area, it is quite possible that the doctor blade will eventually shear the raised area to a point where it will break through the coating, causing a depression instead at that site. Consequently, it will transfer relatively more ink than the surrounding areas and appear as a dark spot in the solid print. When a rubber roll doctoring system is used, it takes longer for the shearing action to be noticed and may camouflage this condition.

The Bottom Line

As soon as the roll begins to show signs of blistering, print quality will suffer. Then, of course, it is time to have the anilox roll re-engraved. Depending on the press design, it may take many hours to change the anilox roll. Added to that is the actual cost of re-engraving a laser anilox roll, which can also be expensive. It could cost thousands of dollars, depending on the size of the roll and line screen.

At this point, what may have seemed like a very minor detail – the pH of the anilox roll cleaning solution – now has become a major concern! What was thought to be a totally safe chemical cleaner that would help keep anilox rolls operating at peak efficiency has now become the very thing that caused the same rolls to fail prematurely.

In light of what has been discussed, it would be helpful if the press personnel keep the following questions in mind and take action if necessary:

• Do I know the pH of my anilox roll cleaner when diluted?

• If so, is it within the safe range (6.0 to 10.5)?

• If not within the safe range, does my anilox roll supplier know about it?

Rigid Maintenance Schedule

Flexographic print quality goes hand-in-hand with how well the press operators are trained. Basic knowledge of the physical – and, in some cases, chemical – properties of the various components of the printing process (such as the anilox rolls, printing plates, inks, substrates and cleaning solutions) ensures better print quality and reduces waste.

Furthermore, following a rigid maintenance schedule for cleaning the anilox rolls and knowing the chemical properties of the cleaning solutions being used are equally important. For instance, selecting the wrong cleaning solution to clean the anilox rolls based on cost alone can be too expensive when compared to the cost of replacing the anilox roll prematurely. Management should see to it that correct practices are applied on the production floor, especially around the presses.

The useful life of the anilox roll is enhanced by proper maintenance procedures. Production supervisors should always be in tune with the various activities around the presses on a daily basis. There is no problem so small that it can be ignored in such an operation, for it could grow into a bigger and more costly one later.

Flexographic printers always strive to prolong the useful life of their anilox rolls by following a rigid schedule in keeping the rolls in excellent condition before and after each printing job. They use the proper cleaning agents and are fully aware of the risk they take when the wrong cleaning solutions are used. Unfortunately, some suppliers of the cleaning solutions ignore the corrosive properties of their products and concentrate mainly on the cleaning effectiveness of the solution. Such products, although they can be good cleaners, often cut short the useful life of the anilox roll. A good cleaning solution must have the right pH in order to clean without harming the anilox roll.

While the pH factor is an important issue, one must also keep in mind other related issues concerning the maintenance of anilox rolls by asking the following questions:

- Do the press operators keep their anilox rolls clean and follow a rigid schedule in cleaning them immediately after every job?

- Do they know the pH of the cleaning solution they use to clean the anilox rolls?

- Do they know the condition of their anilox rolls?

- Do they keep spare rolls for emergencies, and if so, do they know their condition?

- Do they know the cell volume and where to retrieve such information when needed?

Blisters and Cleaner pH Levels

When a corrosive liquid makes its way through the pores of the outer coatings of the anilox roll to the steel base, a localized galvanic cell is formed at that site, triggering a corrosion process. Such localized corrosion normally appears in the form of blisters where the buildup of corrosion products lifts off the coating layer (see *Figure 3*).

Of course, the objective is to clean from the anilox roll any deposits in the cells – mainly, dried inks or coatings. The most important consideration is how to accomplish this task without causing any harm to the anilox roll. Basic knowledge of some critical chemical properties of the cleaners can be extremely helpful in avoiding unnecessary costs down the line.

There is a direct correlation between high cleaning solution pH level and the degree of premature failure of the anilox rolls due to corrosion. Corrosion problems normally occur when the right conditions are present. For example, prolonged exposure of the anilox roll to a high-pH cleaning solution (or any dilution thereof) may cause underfilm corrosion, depending on the composition of the roll.

As the pH of the cleaner approaches either extreme on the pH scale, the chances of encountering corrosion problems become greater. Unfortunately, most suppliers of anilox roll cleaning solutions tend to incorporate in their cleaners high concentrations of strong alkaline ingredients, such as potassium or sodium hydroxide. Such formulation tends to raise the pH of the solution to at least 13 or above.

Figure 4 shows a photomicrograph of an actual blister. The print flaw has a distinct shape, which makes it easily distinguishable from other printing problems. The winged-shape flaw clearly demonstrates the doctor blade action when it passes over a raised blister on the surface of the anilox roll. The doctor blade not only wears out the cells at the blister, but also causes them to carry less ink at that site and allows relatively more ink to deposit at either side of the blister, creating a distinct contrast.

Why Cleaning Solutions Are High pH

The reason cleaning solutions are formulated on the high side of the pH scale is because such solutions are capable of dissolving dried inks and varnishes, as both contain resins. The higher the pH, the better its cleaning action is.

The resins are solid in nature. They can be made soluble in a water-based ink system, however, when the medium is made alkaline by the addition of amines. That is the reason why water-based inks tend to thicken – or increase in viscosity – on the press during hot summer days as the pH of the ink drops below its ideal range, causing the resin to kick out. What actually happens is that as the pH of the system drops, the resin begins to fall out of suspension and agglomerate, forming gel-like lumps in the body of ink or varnish. Normally, this condition is remedied by the careful addition of pH adjuster from time to time to bring the pH of the system back up to the desired alkaline level.

The concept of resolubilizing the dried ink/varnish inside the tiny cells of the anilox roll with highly caustic, strong alkaline cleaning solutions led to its use in formulating the cleaning solution. Of course, the more alkaline the solution, the faster its cleaning action is. Unfortunately, the disadvantage of such cleaning solutions is that they are harmful to the anilox rolls. Although most of the cleaning solutions are alkaline, the ones that have a better chance of survival in the marketplace are those that can do a good cleaning job, yet are not extremely alkaline.

The flexographic printing industry has been saturated with cleaners, especially for cleaning anilox rolls. The need for good anilox roll cleaners is high. The rate of failure is just as high. Listed below are some of the desirable properties of a good anilox roll cleaner:

- user-friendly;

- environmentally friendly;

- aggressive yet not corrosive;

- mildly alkaline or mildly acidic;

- economical.

The pH Factor and the Anilox Roll

With a pH scale of 1 to 14 (1 being highly acidic, 14 highly alkaline and 7 neutral), an extremely alkaline cleaning solution or an extremely acidic solution can be corrosive, providing the right conditions exist. A similar concept applies to inks, as well, when pH adjusters are used at press-side. Although a typical pH range for an ink is between 8.5 and 9.2, careless additions of pH adjusters at press-side can increase the pH of the ink far beyond the recommended range, where it could become harmful to the anilox roll in the long run.

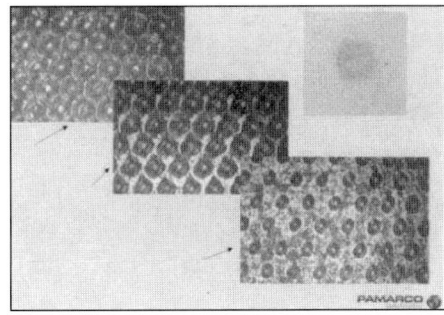

Figure 4. Cell condition at the blistered area and away from it.

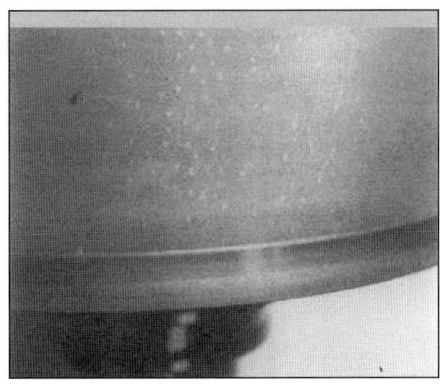

Figure 3. Anilox roll with blisters due to corrosion.

Prolonged contact with a high-alkaline medium may allow ample time for the liquid to penetrate the surface coat to the steel base underneath. Furthermore, while inks with relatively high pH may keep the ink viscosity low in the short run, such a pH level slows down the ink drying rate, causing smearing, poor trapping and, quite often, burnout of the color pigments.

An alkaline cleaning solution with a pH of around 10-10.5 or lower seldom exhibits the tendency to cause corrosion problems during the normal life of the anilox rolls.

The bottom line is that pH solutions on either extreme of the pH scale can cause permanent damage to the anilox roll when the right conditions exist. A good cleaning solution must have the proper pH to be effective, yet cause no harm to the anilox roll itself. ✍

About the authors...
Elias Haddadin is a senior director, technical services, for Pamarco Global Graphics Inc., Atlanta, GA. He has more than 15 years of experience in the flexographic industry, working with ink and anilox roll suppliers. In addition, he has 20 years of technical experience in the metal decorating and can manufacturing areas. Haddadin has participated in FFTA Forums, and was a contributor to the Second Edition of FIRST. He holds an MS degree in physical chemistry and an MBA from Northwestern University.

Art Ruge is a technical sales representative for Pamarco Global Graphics Inc., southeast region (Atlanta, GA). He holds a BA degree in communication from the University of Wisconsin, Parkside. Ruge has 15 years of experience in the flexographic printing field. He is a past contributor to FLEXO as well as a contributor to the Second Edition of FIRST.

DOCTOR-BLADE SENSE

MATERIAL, EDGE TYPE SELECTION BEAR HEAVILY ON PRINT QUALITY

By Ryan F. Platt

While the flexographic printing process has existed for more than 50 years, its ability to achieve consistent, high-quality print that rivals rotogravure and offset print methods is relatively recent. Among the reasons for the significant gain in print quality is the reduction in the amount of ink transferred between anilox, plate and substrate.

Playing an important role in this transformation were higher line counts, resulting from the change to laser ceramic anilox rolls from mechanical engraved chrome; thinner printing plates employing better compressible mounting tapes; and

There are hundreds of factors to consider when using doctor blades on a flexo press. Some factors impact quality, others impact productivity; all impact your cost. Maximizing your production requires that you maximize your doctor blade.

improvements in inks and in chambered blade metering systems. Essentially, with a reduced anilox ink film and less ink in the way, flexo can print cleaner longer.

During this evolution in flexo's process technology, however, little attention has been given to a critical transfer element, the doctor blade. Unlike their counterparts in rotogravure, many flexo print managers still fail to realize the importance of selecting the right blade, and therefore make their selection based upon price, not real value.

Yet consider just how important the metering blade is to your overall success. The right blade can allow you to optimize the process by consistently metering ink on the anilox. Ideally, a blade should seat to the anilox quickly, last a long time and cause little wear and no damage to the anilox roll.

Selection Factors

Selecting the right blade for your application begins by identifying the variables. The following is a list of variables or success factors that should be considered:

- Material: steel or plastic.

- Material consistency.

- Edge: radius, bevel or step (lamella).

- Dimension: length, width and thickness.

- Initial set angle: blade-to-anilox or tangent.

- Contact angle during run (rigidity is important).

- Blade holders: single or chambered.

- Setting the blade in your holder's clamp or extensions.

- Containment blade.

- Interface with end seals.

- Maximizing run times.

- Using the same blade on multiple jobs.

In this article, we will investigate the first three selection factors: steel or plastic material, consistency of material and edge type.

Doctor Blade Material

There are two basic types of doctor blade material used in the flexo industry today: steel and plastic.

While both types have significantly improved over the past few years, there are still very real differences in performance between the two. To understand the importance of these differences, we must be clear about a blade's function.

A doctor blade has one main function: to create and maintain an ink film on an anilox roll so the proper amount of ink can be transferred to the printing plate. It sounds simple until you go deeper.

Thin Material Is Best… Or Is It? One of the breakthrough understandings in the advancement of the flexo process is that a thin ink film on an anilox roll will produce cleaner print longer. When it comes to blades, however, thin blades are not always best, contrary to conventional wisdom. The reason is simple: rigidity. Thin blades are more prone to bending or buckling.

Optimum metering is more related to minimizing a blade's contact area. How much of the blade actually contacts the anilox while metering? When a "thin"

count, cell shape (45-degree, 60-degree or 90-degree channel), the amount of post-laser super-finishing and, of course, the doctor blade material itself are all contributing factors.

The first major factor to be considered when discussing wear and damage is the material itself. Not only is there a difference between plastic and steel materials, but also there are differences within each material group. All steel doctor blades are not the same, and all plastic blades are not the same. The fact is, there are variations in quality—and, ultimately, in performance value—within each material type.

Different Steel Microstructures. Microstructure is one of the important factors determining blade life and anilox roll damage. *Figure 1* and *Figure 2* are photographs of doctor blade materials currently used by flexo printers. They are magnified 1,000 times. These photos clearly illustrate the microstructure differences that can exist from one steel blade to the next.

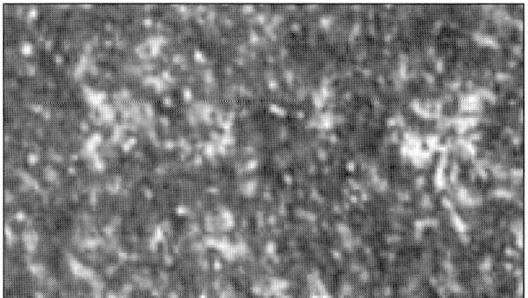

Figure 1

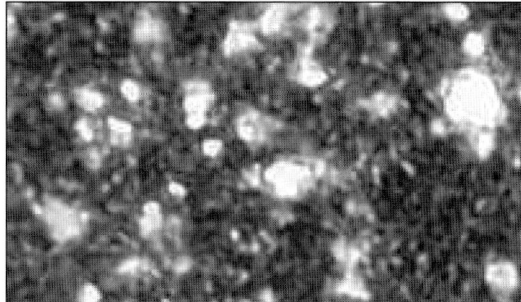

Figure 2

blade is pressed against an anilox, it often bends so its side rather than its tip is doing the metering. When a blade's side is resting against the anilox roll, ink can pass beneath the blade, creating a more-than-desirable ink film. When on its side, a blade will hydroplane. As press speeds increase, so to will the ink film. Dirty print soon follows. When choosing doctor blade material, therefore, thickness of the material and the resulting contact area must be considered.

Steel doctor blades offer the optimal combination of rigidity and thinness to achieve the thinnest ink film. Plastic doctor blades must be four or five times thicker than steel to achieve a similar rigidity. The added material thickness of plastic creates an even wider contact area; therefore, a printer can experience more ink transfer than necessary when using plastic. This additional transfer of ink can cause ink to "wrap around" the dot on the plate material and transfer to the substrate, resulting in dirty print and increased waste.

Material Type Influences Blade and Anilox Roll Wear and Damage. There are many factors that contribute to blade and anilox roll wear and damage. Blade-to-anilox set angle, load pressure, types of inks, anilox roll line

When it comes to microstructure, industry experience suggests that steel containing a finer, more concentrated structure (shown in *Figure 1*) will wear in a more desirable way. On the other hand, experience suggests that steel consisting of a coarser, less populated structure will often cause problems. A blade with the larger, "chunk"-style microstructure shown in *Figure 2* will likely wear faster (resulting in shorter blade life), provide a less consistent metering edge and allow for larger particles to enter the ink system. It is these particles that can cause lines in your print and cause damage or score lines on the anilox roll—ouch!

Material Consistency

Consistency is a topic that is rarely discussed when talking about blades, but one that can have monumental impact. It is critical that a printer has confidence that each doctor blade used is of the same quality and the same microstructure. If he does, he can reasonably expect to produce print of the same quality and consistency regardless of when the blades were purchased.

Just think of the ramifications of doctor blade material consistency when an important customer calls needing a rush job. All your resources are directed toward satisfying that job. The job is set and ready to run. The job begins. Partway through the run, however, there is a color failure, or major streaks appear in the print. The job stops. You fail to meet the deadline. An investigation determines that the blade failed. How many times would further investigation of the blade material's microstructure reveal inconsistency?

Certified Quality and Consistency. Your customers demand it; why shouldn't you? Once you have settled on the right material, ask your supplier for material quality certification. Can the supplier provide proof that what he/she agrees to supply today will be the same as what you get tomorrow or next year?

The Edge of a Doctor Blade

Doctor blades are designed with three basic edges: lamella, bevel and radius. The lamella (or "stepped") edge was originally designed for the rotogravure printing industry. In gravure, the blade is set to wipe the cylinder. The stepped edge flexes, allowing the operator to make on-press adjustments to overcome print

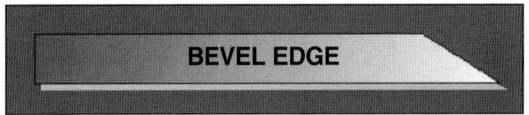

issues as they arise.

In flexo, however, a blade is set in a reverse angle to the anilox, not in

a wiping angle. To be effective, a blade must scrape or sheer excess ink from the anilox. The tip should remain rigid, with no flex. In many flexo applications, excessive blade-to-anilox pressure can cause the stepped edge to snap. Concerns for smooth blade seating can be dealt with effectively with higher-quality materials and improved, more durable tips. The bottom line is that the lamella edge is the most expensive, offering little or no advantage for most flexo applications.

The bevel edge is very successful in situations that demand an immediate blade-to-anilox roll seat. The bevel allows the blade to contact the anilox roll at a specific point, causing a proper wipe of the anilox roll from the beginning of each run. The one negative aspect of this blade is that as it wears, the amount of steel in contact with the anilox roll increases until it stabilizes when it reaches full gauge (the time at which the bevel is completely worn). The continual change in the amount of contact area changes the wipe of the anilox roll, thereby changing the ink film and possibly the color of the printed product. This edge is most popular in narrow-web and non-chambered applications.

Since 1996, the radius edge blade has become the most popular edge used in flexo. Usually, this type of blade is rounded on each edge. One benefit of the radius edge is the fact that by having the exact same edge on each side of the blade, there is no wrong way to install the blade in the holder. There is no front or back side. Either edge can be placed into the clamp or against the anilox.

Another big benefit is safety. It is much safer to handle a radius edge than other edges during installation. There is no "sharp" edge. Caution should be taken, however, during installation and removal after use. When seating to the anilox, the blade's radius makes contact with the anilox's surface radius edge at one place. This edge, when coupled with highly-structured steel, quickly conforms to the anilox, establishing a constant contact area. This enables the blade to be run at full gauge for basically the entire run. Consistency of wipe, consistent ink transfer and consistent color are more easily achieved. Those using a radius edge report extended blade life when compared to a lamella or a bevel edge.

Just the Beginning

How often do you hear, "The devil is in the details"? Nothing could be truer when it comes to doctor blades. There are hundreds of factors to consider when using doctor blades on a flexo press. Some factors impact quality, others impact productivity; all impact your cost. Maximizing your pro-

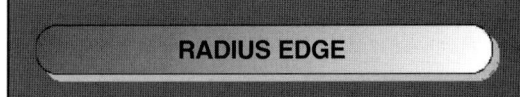

duction requires that you maximize your doctor blade. Just identifying all the variables is a daunting challenge for most printers. That's why it is important for a printer to choose a full-service blade supplier.

Ideally, in addition to offering the best possible materials selection, your blade supplier should be able to "audit" your pressroom to assess compliance with all blade-related principles and practices. Your blade supplier should be able to present a detailed assessment report, make process improvement recommendations, assist with training and implementation of changes if necessary and provide follow-up compliance audits.

About the Author:
Ryan F. Platt is an area manager for Charlotte, NC-based FLXON Inc. He provides technical support and training to flexo and gravure printers in both the U.S. and Canada. Platt, who has been working in the industry for more than five years, holds a bachelor's degree in economics and international studies from Wake Forest University and a master's degree in business administration from Colorado State University.

ELIMINATING THE PHOTOPOLYMER PLATE VARIABLE

TROUBLESHOOTING PRINT PROBLEMS
ALL COMES DOWN TO QUALITY CONTROL

If you've been making plates for a long time, getting back to the basics can help a great deal in preventing mistakes. Producing a high-quality plate the first time goes a long way in shortening the troubleshooting process.

By Charlotte Cushing

Sometimes you make a bad plate; it happens. Knowing what went wrong and how to fix it quickly is important in today's environment, where we all have so little time and much more to do. Plate performance can usually be traced to changes in prepress, platemaking conditions or press techniques. Errors in platemaking can cost valuable press time and money!

If you've been making plates for a long time, getting back to the basics can help a great deal in preventing mistakes. Producing a high-quality plate the first time goes a long way in shortening the troubleshooting process.

First of all, your plate manufacturer can assist you by supplying a few essential tools to help you release a good-quality plate from the plateroom. Take advantage of these quality tools or information they offer. Tools to document your process, tools to organize, checklists, process control tools and troubleshooting information are available.

Many of us have experienced the same problem when it comes to platemaking capabilities and processing. Some of the well-known issues may be documented in plate-manufacturer-issued technical bulletins or troubleshooting guides. Ask your plate manufacturer or check on its website in order to have these tools handy as a quick ref-

A platemaker examines the image quality of a new plate.

Photo courtesy of of DuPont Imaging Technologies

erence. If your plate manufacturer does not have what you need, communicate that fact to the manufacturer; company representatives will be more than happy to help you.

High-Quality Plate Requirements

What are the prerequisites for making and releasing a good-quality plate? Below is a brief list:

• A trained and qualified platemaker.

• Recommended film or digital file specifications.

• Optimized times for all steps in making the plate (step tests).

• Process control tools (production log, quality check list, control strip).

Step tests are performed to optimize the back exposure, main exposure and even the light finishing.

- A preventive equipment-maintenance program.

- Maintaining correct washout solution balance.

- Good housekeeping.

- Additional quality tools, such as a micrometer and flexo dot analyzers.

There are times—even if you feel that you've made a good plate—when it still comes back from the pressroom. The press operators are blaming a printing problem on the plate, and say they need a new one made right away. The first step you must take is to find out where the process went wrong. Could it be a bad plate, or could it be a prepress, ink or press problem?

Checklist For Quality

If you did not QC your plate before releasing it, you will now need to take the time to determine if the plate is bad. Below is a list of basic checks needed to assess the quality of your photopolymer plate.

- **Were the films or digital file checked for correct specifications and dot size?** Films should be checked before imaging the plate. You should also confirm that the bitmapped output file is correct. If the film or digital file specifications are incorrect, all of your platemaking efforts will not produce a sharply-imaged or high-quality plate.

- **Are all the required dots held on the plate?** Was the exposure time optimized for this job? Insufficient exposure will affect dot formation and can cause dirty printing. Too much exposure could cause dots to chip or could cause excessive dot gain.

- **Are the reverses open, and are the lines straight?** If your reverses are not deep enough, it might mean you are overexposing the plate or using incorrect film specifications. This would cause poor printing.

- **For analog plates, are there any "out of contact" spots—fat type, filled-in reverses, shiny spots?** If you see any "out of contact" spots, this could indicate incorrect matte level on your film, poor vacuum or poor platemaking technique. This will also cause poor printing.

- **Did you check the plate for artifacts, pinholes, solvent spots, chipping, cracks?** Any of these will print!

- **Is the surface of the plate tacky?** If you have not properly finished the plate, dirty printing can occur. Different plate types may have different finishing times.

- **Did you measure the plate before releasing it to determine if it was dried down completely, of uniform thickness and with the proper relief?** An uneven plate will cause high/low spots in the print. It could also indicate that a plate has swollen on press due to ink/solvent incompatibility. It is important to have a micrometer.

- **Is the plate washed down to a true floor?** If not, your process dots may not be supported properly, causing them to break.

- **Did you check the control strip for correct dot size or gain?** Using an instrument to read dots imaged on a control strip can confirm that various-size dots have been imaged on the plate, and to what degree of dot gain—negative to plate—you are dealing with.

- **Was the plate cleanly trimmed and beveled?** A properly trimmed and beveled plate will prevent any kinks, nicks or jagged edges that would ruin the plate during mounting and repositioning; allow ink to penetrate between the polyester support base and the polymer; or cause the plate to lift from the cylinder.

Systematically evaluating each area listed above—before the plate is sent to press—is your best chance of minimizing the number of defective plates sent back to the plateroom or returned from your customer. Investigating process-of-use issues after the fact can be a time-consuming task. Establishing quality controls in the plateroom will save time in the long run, add value to your business and eliminate the plate as a variable in printing situations.

ABOUT THE AUTHOR:
Charlotte Cushing is senior technical service analyst for DuPont Imaging Technologies, Wilmington, DE. For more information regarding Cyrel® printing plates, platemaking equipment or color proofing systems, contact her at charlotte.m.cushing@usa.dupont.com or call 800-345-9999.

PRESS SLEEVE BASICS

RAW MATERIALS & CONSTRUCTION ARE KEY TO LONG SERVICE LIFE

To ensure high printing quality, the surface hardness should be adapted to the particular application concerned.

The innermost sleeve layer, usually comprising glass-fiber-reinforced plastic (GFK), must ensure an absolutely non-slip seat and at the same time enable mounting onto the cylinder through certain expandability. Photos by Klemens Ehrlitzer

By Klemens Ehrlitzer

For the cursory observer, the simple geometrical form of a hollow cylinder suggests that a flexo plate sleeve is a simple product. In practice, however, the sleeve turns out to be a technically highly-developed precision part that plays a key role in the printing process. An enormous amount of specialist know-how that simply cannot be seen with the naked eye goes into sleeve production.

The essential quality criteria are defined by the materials and production processes implemented. Presses demand a great deal from sleeves. The requirements made on the material may be extremely stringent and sometimes even contrary, depending on the function to be fulfilled. For example, a good sleeve should guarantee both easy mounting onto the carrier cylinder and—at the same time—an absolutely secure seat during production.

A sleeve should also be able to compensate for any deformation processes resulting from the centrifugal and impact forces arising in the press. Cut- and shock-proof ability, as well as resistance to chemicals, are important properties for the surface of the sleeve.

A sleeve can meet users' expectations regarding long service life, production reliability and printing quality only if suitable raw materials and manufacturing processes are implemented in its production. Following is a brief description of the construction of the sleeve's layers, and their function.

Innermost Layer

The innermost layer of a sleeve is in direct contact with the carrier cylinder. It is generally composed of glass-fiber-reinforced plastic (GFK) and basically has to fulfill two requirements. First, it must ensure an absolutely non-slip seat. The fast-as-possible bonding with the carrier cylinder is an absolute must for the sleeve to be able to do its job during the printing process.

At the same time, however, the GFK layer must be expandable in order to enable the sleeve to be mounted onto the cylinder. Because production reliability enjoys top priority in the printing world, compromises that merely simplify sleeve mounting are unacceptable.

The thicker the GFK layer, the more compressed the air must be, to enable the sleeve to be mounted on a press. With a certain layer thickness, the compressed air required is so voluminous that mounting turns into a safety hazard. This occurs with basic sleeves made of glass fiber with a thickness of approximately 2 mm and with coated sleeves that are approximately 5 mm thick. The pressure load, moreover, leads to excess stress on the material, which, in turn, affects the continuous clamping capacity on the air cylinder. For this reason, the GFK layer in multi-layered sleeves should be limited to a wall thickness of approximately 2.5 mm to 3 mm.

Compressible Inner Layer

To compensate for expansion in such sleeve layers, some manufacturers implement a compressible layer on top of the inner GFK layer. This compressible material is capable of resuming its original state within as short a time as possible after being expanded by the mounting procedure.

If there is not such a layer with defined compressibility, expansion will occur in an uncontrolled manner throughout the entire material surrounding the GFK layer. This places particular strain at the weakest points of the material, leading to premature fatigue. Therefore, to ensure that the product remains in perfect working order and has a long service life, users should select sleeves with a compressible inner layer covering the GFK layer.

Materials Make a Difference

Because different materials and production methods are implemented in printing, there are very great differences in quality among the various sleeves available on the market.

A sleeve's layers must not individually accommodate high loads during the printing process. The centrifugal forces resulting from the rotation movement as well as the impact force—incurred especially at the printing-plate edge—act on the layers' bonding with extreme force. This makes tremendous demands on the bond between the various materials. Furthermore, these forces also deform the compressible inner layer. A printing result with satisfactory quality is dependent on the material's recovery within one revolution. This requires particularly high-performance materials.

Polyurethane foam is the preferred raw material for the compressible inner layer. It comes in rolls, and is fitted by the manufacturer onto the sleeve as a tape and adhered there. The layer obtains its final properties in the course of further processing. Because of the higher production and materials costs, an alternative process

The sleeve surface is most subjected to external influences. Printing plants should therefore pay special attention to products with a resistant outer layer.

is sometimes used, in which a polyurethane material is foamed directly onto the inner sleeve and subsequently compacted. This process makes for more inexpensive production, but the resulting sleeves cannot match the high-grade properties of the first method, and have a shorter service life.

A sleeve made of polyurethane material has an extremely compressible volume. As a result, a compressible inner layer with a thickness between 1.5 and 2.0 mm is sufficient for conventional form sleeves to take up the entire expansion of the inner sleeve during the mounting procedure. The consequence is exactly defined compression only in this area, the layers above not being affected.

Just as important as compressibility is the recovery capacity of this layer. As soon as the carrier cylinder's compressed-air pad is switched off, the polyurethane must resume its original state very rapidly. For practical applications, the stability of this layer in a non-compressed state is of decisive importance.

Intermediary Layer

The build-up or intermediary layer follows the inner compressible layer. The material used here is likewise polyurethane. In this case, stability is the most important property. For that reason, filled polyurethane as well as foamed polyurethane are used in the intermediary layer. Because there is a tendency in current development toward lighter-weight sleeves, a

Polyurethane is implemented for manufacturing sleeves in varied forms.

complete change to foamed materials is expected in the long run.

This trend answers printing press market demands for presses with eight and more printing units as well as wider printing widths. For operators to be able to deal with the form sleeves simply and safely, their weight must be correspondingly adapted to the new situation. This is usually achieved by hollows or cavities within the plastics employed. Because stability is diminished as raw material density is reduced, however, there is only limited scope for lowering sleeve weight.

Sleeve Surface

Of special significance for practical application is the sleeve surface, as it is most subjected to external influences. Printing plants should therefore pay special attention to implementing products with a resistant outer layer. Such sleeves should be impact-proof to avoid damage when butted in transport or upset in storage. Even if cutting adhesive tape or plates on the sleeve surface is to be avoided as a matter of principle, the material should still be able to withstand this stress.

The bonding properties of the sleeve surface also play a decisive role in the interplay with adhesive tape. Adhesive tape manufacturers have developed a wide range of different products in the past few years. For printing plants, the market offers a great variety of just the right adhesive tape for all conventional fields of application and combinations of sleeve and printing plate. In fact, the spectrum has become so comprehensive that a great deal of experience is needed to make the right selection.

Preventing Blistering

One problem some users complain of is blistering between the adhesive tape and sleeve. Blistering is sometimes caused by gas generation, which can be avoided when the sleeve is manufactured with cross-linked polyurethane. Gas-generation is very slight if, in raw material production, the appropriate manufacturing method is implemented and the proportion of basic chemicals used is accurate. Should the composition of the various constituents deviate from the optimum value, however, carbon dioxide (a common cause of blistering) can be observed to form under the influence of atmospheric moisture.

Alongside conventional polyurethane materials, sleeves are also available with resin-based surfaces. Through use, they may absorb considerable adhesive or become porous. In either case, handling is affected. Above all, when printing plates are being dismantled, the bond between the plate and adhesive tape may be released only with difficulty, so that any remainder of the adhesive tape must be laboriously removed from the sleeve.

Surface Hardness & Application

Another important element for high printing quality is adaptation of surface hardness to the particular application. The surface hardness can be selected as a function of the plate types used and the substrates to be printed on.

Sleeves with a hard surface are preferred for film or foil printing, which requires adequate printing pressure. Products with medium hardness are used for such applications as paper napkins. Soft surfaces are meant especially for either very rough substrates or when very fine gradations are to be printed.

Improving Production Conditions

Another aspect affecting sleeve quality is the production conditions. Fluctuations in manufacturing-plant temperatures caused merely by changing seasons may cause unacceptable dimensional deviations in plastics due to the thermal expansion factor.

Sleeve production must be maintained under constant conditions regarding temperature and atmospheric moisture. This ensures, for example, that sleeves maintain the diameter required. This procedure will be extended even further in the future to include dust control.

About the Author:
Klemens Ehrlitzer is a freelance journalist who covers the printing industry. He is the former chief editor of the German magazine Flexoprint, official journal of the DFTA.

Photo by Klemens Ehrlitzer

Choosing Mounting Plate Tape

Correct Tape Selection Can Reduce Down Time Caused by Trapped Air

Diagrams A, B & C

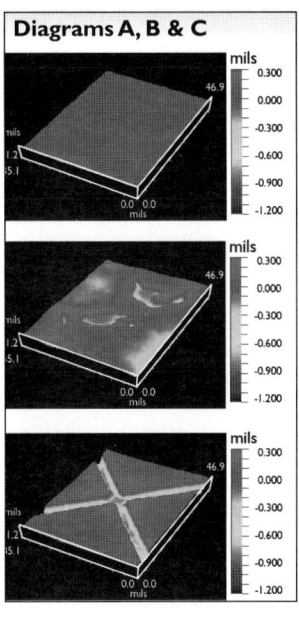

By Brian Burquest

For the past several years, a trend toward improved print quality and consistency has driven the flexo industry. This trend has been stimulated by the demands of flexo print buyers who are looking for better overall images. At the same time, competition and an economic downturn have exacerbated the need to drive down costs. The result: a broad range of new technologies to address these market demands.

Beyond plate and press improvements, the printer's general direction is to consider thinner plates and tapes in addition to specific tape densities suited for the desired print result. We also are beginning to see process color systems with more than four colors replacing the traditional CMYK systems.

Faster platemaking processes and off-the-shelf "in-the-round" systems are current approaches targeting productivity improvements and the reduction of overall costs to take a job from the proof to the finished jumbo of material.

Unfortunately, many printers have overlooked some other approaches related to how plates are mounted. Subtle but important improvements in mounting-tape products can help to optimize mounting procedures while facilitating the highest possible print quality results.

The mounting process consists of both tape and plate mounting. Inherent to each step is the risk of entrapping air. This risk calls for extra care during the mounting process. Air entrapment occurs during both tape and plate mounting. Tiny pockets of air can be trapped between the tape and cylinder or sleeve as well as between the printing plate and the mounting tape. These pockets of air tend to migrate while on press, forming hard air bubbles that translate into high spots on the plate image.

If an air bubble were to settle underneath a print area of the plate, it would be strong enough to deform the plate, causing a high spot in the image. These high or dense spots – if unnoticed through mounting and proofing – will almost certainly result in press downtime as the operator troubleshoots the print defect. If unnoticed through printing, the result will be poor print quality and quite possibly the rejection of that job. The bottom line is that air entrapment costs money.

Types of Tape Liner

A typical mounting tape is comprised of foam, cylinder and plate-side adhesives as well as a product liner. There often is very little thought put into what the liner actually does for the mounting tape. Throughout the years, tape manufacturers have developed liner technologies that have attempted to combat the problem of air entrapment. Here we will examine three of these technologies and how they try to eliminate this problem.

The pebbled liner, as the name suggests, has a rough, random-embossed pattern, which imparts a rough, pebbled texture onto the adhesive surface. It is typically constructed of polypropylene and was developed in the 1980s.

The flat or smooth liner is usually a poly-coated

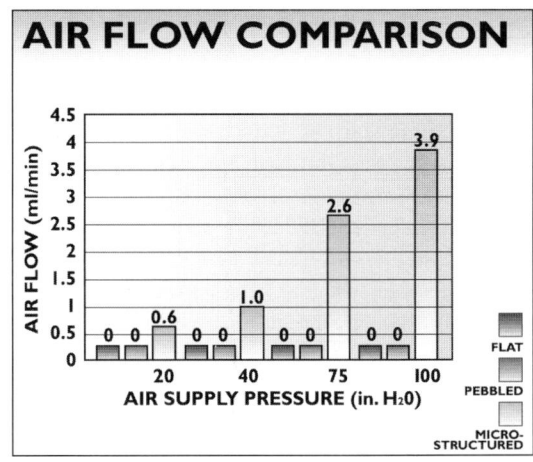

paper or polyester construction. This approach to incorporate stiffer liners to combat air entrapment was first attempted in the 1990s. This liner is also the most common in the market today.

Finally, the micro-structured liner is a new, patented technology. It consists of a continuous crosshatched ridge pattern that is embossed into the liner. This pattern creates continuous channels in the adhesive surface.

Comparing Adhesive Surfaces

It is actually the adhesive surface – not the liner – that affects air entrapment. Each unique product liner imparts a different pattern onto the adhesive surface. To understand how these surfaces impact air entrapment, each of the different adhesive surface patterns was examined with an optical profiler.

This device utilizes Vertical Scanning Interferometry

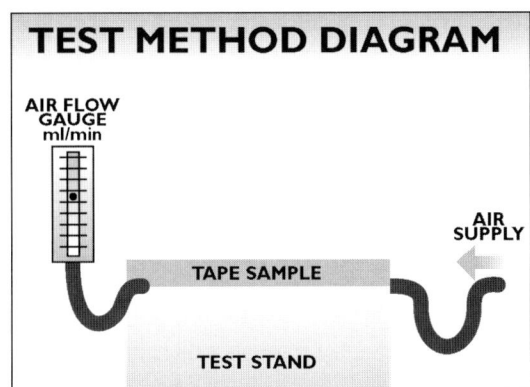

(VSI) technology to visually characterize the adhesive surface topography of each tape sample. *Image A* shows the adhesive surface of the flat linered material. Notice the legend on the right utilizes a spectral range of colors to characterize the differences in surface heights. The units of measurement are in mils, or thousandths of an inch. Also notice the dimensions of the sample are 47 x 35 mils in size. The flat liner imparts a relatively flat surface on the adhesive. Typical peak-to-valley variation for this adhesive is only 5 hundredths of a mil.

Image B shows the adhesive surface of the pebbled liner. This view depicts the pits and ridges that are formed by the pebbled liner. You can also see larger areas – independent of the defined pits and valleys – that have significant contour changes. The key element of this image is that there are no continuous paths on this surface for air to flow. Air can be trapped within these random structures. The pits and valleys are, on average, 13-14 mils wide with a depth of 0.5- 0.6 mils.

Finally, the micro-structured adhesive surface (shown in *Image C*) is a continuous network of crosshatched channels through which air can travel. The widths of these channels are typically 4 mils wide with a depth of approximately 1 mil. Here again, the adhesive surface adjacent to each channel is very uniform and essential-

ly flat. The permanent, continuous channels allow air to flow from underneath the plate and tape.

Testing for Air Entrapment

In order to understand how air entrapment affects tape mounting, each tape was mounted to a Plexiglas panel and then a 0.067-inch photopolymer plate was applied. The plate was rolled down with a 4.5-lb. roller to ensure uniform mounting pressure. Pictures were taken of the results through the plate floor and solid areas.

Figure 1 shows the flat liner sample. The image on the left is through the plate floor; the image on the right is through a solid printing area. Observe the white (lighter) areas. These indicate where the adhesive and the plate are not in contact because air has been trapped during the mounting process.

Look at the same images of the pebbled liner sample in *Figure 2*. Note the many random pockets of air. The pits and valleys created by the liner on the adhesive surface actually trap air underneath the plate within these structures.

The micro-structured tape in *Figure 3* has a significantly higher surface area contact than the previous two examples. Note that the crosshatch pattern makes up the majority of the non-contact area. Other than the crosshatch channels, there are very few non-contact areas. If you look hard enough, the crosshatch pattern is still visible underneath the solid plate area.

A test method was developed to quantify and substantiate these visual observations. Below is a diagram of the apparatus used to conduct this test. The tape sample is mounted to the steel platen surface of the test stand with air fittings to introduce air underneath the tape. Air is actually pumped below the surface of a mounted tape. The amount of airflow is then measured in ml/min., as the air is bled to the other side.

The graph (page 47) displays the results. Notice that the only samples showing air bleed or flow capability are those with the micro-structured liner. This graph also shows that as the air supply pressure rises, the airflow also increases. These results correspond with our visual observations.

What does all this data mean to the flexo printer? Air entrapment can cause unnecessary delays and risks to your business. A micro-structured liner can significantly reduce your chances of entrapping air in the mounting process.

Your choice of mounting tape can have a significant impact on your ability to meet the demands of the market while maintaining or reducing costs. Choose a tape that will effectively streamline your process and increase the consistency of your print quality.

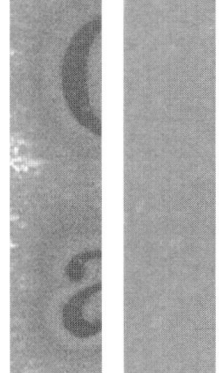
Figure 1. Standard Plate Floor (left) and Solid Plate.

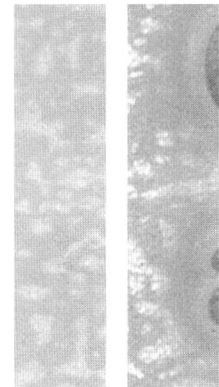
Figure 2. Pebbled Plate Floor (left) and Solid Plate.

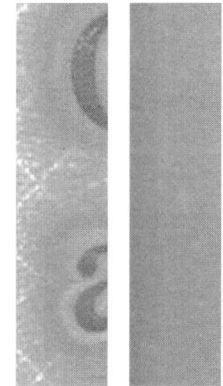
Figure 3: Microstructured Plate Floor (left) and Solid Plate.

About the Author:
Brian Burquest is senior technical service engineer for 3M Co., Industrial Tape and Specialties Division, St. Paul, MN.

One-Shot Design
Communication Is Key to Getting It Right the First Time

By Michael Paeth

Flexo has come a long way. There have been advances in presses, inks, platemaking, anilox rolls, materials and just about every facet of this industry. The ability to print complex designs using four-color process and spot colors at high line screens has evolved from a dream into a daily reality. Flexo is now competing in industries as diverse as labels and tags, pouches, cartons and boxes, balloons, bottle and can wraps and an endless list of flexible packaging niches. Flexo is also competing against offset and gravure – and beating them hands down.

One area of this industry that continually seems to lag behind is design at the prepress end of the chain. A large percentage of designs cannot be separated or printed the way they were initially set up. Many designers seem to rarely know what method is being used to print the job.

While flexo can be one of the most flexible printing processes, it has inherent limitations. In addition, many designers don't take full benefit of the advantages that flexo has to offer. In the end, most designs that are reworked are done at considerable cost to the customer. And just about all reworking of art is completely avoidable by having open communication and following basic guidelines.

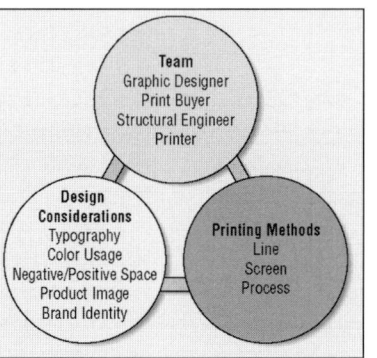

A successful flexo printed piece results from a team effort that works within the parameters of design considerations and printing processes.

Basic Rules of Design

In the last decade, the personal computer has taken over graphic design and prepress. The keyboard and mouse have replaced the rubylith, lithograph pens, triangles and T-squares. A lot of the old rules went out with the old tools, supplanted by an "it's on the disk" mentality. This line of thinking worked for a while. But then in came on-demand printing and just-in-time printing. Now designs need to work the first time, because prepress departments and printing companies have less time.

Here are 10 golden rules of design that should be adhered to regardless of the printing process or time frame for completing a job.

1. *Software.* If you are creating artwork in any program other than Quark, PageMaker, Illustrator, Freehand or PhotoShop, make a phone call first. These programs are the universally accepted software applications used by 95 percent of all prepress establishments. If you are using any other software, call your printer and make sure he or she can accept the file.

2. *Mac or IBM.* Most prepress departments are Macintosh-based. Some can accept IBM-formatted disks; some cannot. If you are working on an IBM computer, call and see if the prepress department can accept your disk.

3. *Supply a backup copy.* It is always best to supply a duplicate file on a second disk. CDs, zip disks and floppies can get damaged in shipping. It takes a few extra minutes, but in the long run it could save an entire day.

4. *E-mail etiquette.* When sending a file via the Internet, give as much information as possible in your e-mail cover letter. We still receive many files without so much as a note saying what the file is for or whom it's from.

5. *Supply a disk reference sheet.* Outputting a disk reference showing exactly what is on the disk and the names of files is extremely helpful to prepress operators.

6. *Output composite and separated lasers.* Before sending out a disk, output a set of laser proofs. This will give the prepress operator something to check the file against. If you have access to a color laser printer, a color comp will always be appreciated.

7. *Fonts.* Unless you don't mind font substitution and text re-flow, always supply your printer and screen fonts.

8. *Scans.* If you have imported scans, make sure to mark them either as "FPO" (for position only) or intended for final output. Also make sure the resolution of the file is high enough. The minimum for grayscale or color photos is usually 300 dpi, while 1200 dpi is a good resolution for line art. Remember that if you scan something at 300 dpi and enlarge it 200 percent in Quark or Illustrator, you just made the effective resolution of the file 150 dpi—which is no longer sufficient.

9. *Trapping.* Unless you have an agreement with your prepress supplier, do not trap the files yourself. If you do, the prepress house will probably go through and re-trap the file anyway, so you are not saving any time or money.

10. *Proofing.* Expect the prepress provider to send a proof back to you. Unless the prepress house has an understanding with you, they will usually want you to sign off on some sort of proof. This is to protect them – and you.

A Proactive Approach

When creating graphics that will be printed on a flexographic printing press, there are several things that need to be taken into account. When a designer creates a design that maximizes the benefits of flexo – while designing around its limitations – the results can be outstanding. If the designer ignores the "rules" of designing for flexo, the opposite can be true – or the prepress house ends up totally rebuilding the file.

A good design starts before the final artwork files are even put together. An open chain of communication between designer, prepress and printing is the key to make any design work. Prepress usually knows what the printer can and cannot print. The good prepress manager should also be the liaison between the printer and designer, and should be utilized as such. It is a good idea to send the prepress department a design early on, so staff can spot any potential problems and make suggestions for alterations. This is especially true if there will be multiple "flavors" of the same design. This proactive approach helps minimize any re-work, before multiple designs are produced.

Know Your Press

Knowing what the press capability is will always be a benefit. Flexo printers rarely run a four-color process job as just a four-color process. Many times, the halftone portion of the black separation is printed on a separate print station from any black line copy or line art. This allows the press operator to keep a rich, dark black for heavy solid areas without dirtying up the screened portion of the job. Sometimes a large area of color will be separated out as spot color. If you couple this with spot colors that may already exist in the design, the number of needed print stations grows quickly.

While presses can accommodate as many as 10 colors, six to eight colors is usually the maximum that can be utilized. Also remember that if a job is being varnished, that process will take up one of those print stations. If a job is being printed on foil, a white ink plate may be needed, too.

Know what line screen the press is capable of. A line screen of 133 was a long-running standard for flexo, but 150 is quickly becoming the standard, and 175 to 200 line is not unheard of anymore. Obviously, the higher the line screen, the more attractive the results. And the smaller the graphics, the higher the line screen needed to give the most detail. The maximum line screen that can be printed on a particular press is primarily determined by the selection of anilox rolls available.

The size, depth and frequency of the honeycomb pattern on the anilox roll directly affects how much ink is transferred to the plate. A finer-line anilox (700 to 1,000 line, typically) is used for printing 133 to 175 line process. A coarser-line anilox (300 to 600) is typically used for coarser screens and solids. The best way to find the maximum line screen that can be printed on a certain press is to first find out the maximum line screen that is available for a full set of anilox rollers for the intended press. Take this number and divide by 5. (For example: 1,000 line anilox divided by 5 = 200 line screen.) This will give you an approximate maximum line screen that can be printed using this anilox.

While a finer-line anilox gives a nice, thin film of ink to print very fine halftone screens, a fine-line anilox is not good for printing large, solid blocks of color. If the prepress staff has not foreseen the potential problem, the press operator may be forced to either use a fine-line anilox to keep the screens clean and sharp, leaving large solid areas of colors looking somewhat lighter and washed out; or to use a coarser anilox to keep large blocks of color nice and dark, sacrificing the screens, leaving them a bit more plugged up. If the halftone screens and the solid color blocks can be isolated onto separate print stations, the best of both worlds can be achieved.

Changing an anilox to a different screen frequency is the primary way a press operator can remove an unwanted cast of color within a design. If flesh tones look a bit red, changing to a finer anilox on the magenta print deck can help remove the unwanted cast. Changing an anilox yields a global change, so while a red cast may have been removed from the flesh tones, the magenta was also lightened everywhere else in the design.

Concept Proof
Indicates layout of graphic elements.
Not intended for use as a target for color matching.

Contract Proof
Indicates layout of graphic elements.
Intended for use as a target for color matching.

The concept proof is used to indicate alignment of graphic elements in the package layout, while the contract proof is used to show accuracy in color.

Know Your Substrate

The substrate used is a primary factor in the overall "finish" of a job. Designers, unfortunately, are not kept in the loop when a specific substrate is chosen. Factors other than printability may be at play when a substrate is chosen, and the design can suffer because of it.

Flexo printers use a wide variety of label stock, film, foil, tag stock and coarse materials. Some are not suited for printing fine line screens and process work. Many thin films need increased trapping considerations. Some paper-coated foils have a blue-gray or yellow cast that affects process printing. A designer should be proactive in finding out what substrate will be used for a job.

Most converters have used a wide variety of substrates, and know the pitfalls and limitations for all of the substrates that they use. Because they want a nice-looking finished piece, too, most are happy to give information regarding the printability of a specific substrate.

Flexo Printing Factors

Because flexography is a form of letterpress printing, it has inherent limitations. These can be compounded by ink, substrate, press and prepress/plate limitations. Keep the following in mind when designing for flexo.

Print Element Growth. Because flexo printing uses a photopolymer (or occasionally rubber) printing plate, print element growth is a fact of life. Photopolymer has improved dramatically in the past two decades. Direct-to-plate and high-definition platemaking has also reduced press gain. There are, however, a few things to be aware of. Try to keep reversed-out type above 6 pt. in size. Reversed-out type below 10 pt. is best in a bold, san-serif typeface. Any other small, reversed graphics and lines should be kept as bold and open as possible.

Vignettes. Vignettes can occasionally be a challenge to print, depending on press conditions, substrate, plate and ink type. The best idea is to talk with the converter about his ability to print clean and smooth vignettes, and design the job accordingly.

Some converters prefer that vignettes "point" in a direction opposite to the printed web. Others prefer vignettes be printed at a coarser line screen. Look at samples of previously printed vignettes to get a better idea of what is possible – and what isn't. A photopolymer plate can generally hold a minimum 3 percent dot. (High-definition and direct-to-plate has improved on this minimum.) This 3 percent dot will grow to anywhere from 6 percent to 10 percent, depending on press conditions. So, it is theoretically impossible to have a vignette fade into the white background without seeing a hard line. The best solution to this "hard line" effect is to hide where the vignette ends. For example, the light end of a vignette can be hidden by ending it in the bleed area of the art; or another graphic element (a block of color, a line or a line of type) can cover where the vignette ends.

Special Inks. Some converters have certain limitations when it comes to special inks like metallics and fluorescents, which generally cannot be printed with fine line screens due to their pigments. Fluorescent

inks also tend to dry faster. This means the press operator may need to run the job faster to keep the ink from drying on the plate before it can be transferred to the paper. Find out from the converter if he has any limitations when it comes to specialty inks. Also keep in mind that flexo inks are, for the most part, transparent. If you specify a block of magenta to print directly onto a block of yellow, you will end up with a color close to PMS 1795.

Trapping. Trapping is best defined as the overlapping of two adjacent colors to avoid any misregistration of colors on press. Misregistration occurs due to material slip and stretch, differences in plate-mounting techniques and press tolerances. For flexo printing, .01-inch is considered a standard trap. Depending on the job, more or less trap may be specified.

Trapping is best left to the prepress department that will be plating the job. Because trapping can have a negative effect on the overall look of the job, however, designers need to keep trapping in mind. For example, because flexo inks are transparent, if there is a block of PMS 185 red next to a block of PMS 348 green, the resulting trap will yield a brown trap line.

Printing Plate Limitations. Photopolymer has been one of the most improved-upon parts of flexographic printing. One limitation is its inability to hold very fine highlight dot. Another is its need to be wrapped around a print cylinder, creating a visible seam where the two ends of the plate meet. If there are no graphics present in the seam area, there is no issue; if there are, those graphics may need to be adjusted to accommodate the seam. There is technology available for a seamless plate, but not every job can justify its high price tag.

Software. Most flexographic prepress departments and trade shops use the universally accepted Adobe Illustrator and Macromedia Freehand for production and file assembly. While some will accept and work with Quark Xpress documents, many will rebuild the files in Freehand or Illustrator. The same is true for Adobe PageMaker and Corel Draw documents. The jury is still out on Adobe Indesign, as this program is still fairly new. Freehand and Illustrator are much more sophisticated production tools, and handle the intricacies of trapping for flexo much better than Quark or PageMaker.

Designing for flexo has a fairly steep learning curve. The key to getting it right the first time is communication. Prepress trade shops and flexographic converters are usually more than happy to share information to help make the final product that much more appealing.

About the Author...
Michael Paeth is the owner of FlexoGrafix, Glendale Heights, IL, a full-service prepress trade shop specializing in flexo. He can be contacted by phone at 888-824-0400 or by email at flexografx@aol.com

COMPUTER-TO-PLATE CHALLENGE

YOU CAN OVERCOME STUMBLING BLOCKS TO ACHIEVE POSITIVE PRINTING RESULTS

By David Chinnis & Holger Neumann

During the last few years, digital imaging of flexo plates has enjoyed a high growth rate. The supply of lasers – Nd:YAG, diode and fiber types – has increased, as has the variety of plates available. Such quality improvements as high range of contrast, clearly smoother gradations and lower dot gains put flexo close to gravure and offset.

The use of sleeve technology with digital imaging will surely speed up this trend and increase the competition with offset in the folding-carton field, especially as a consequence of in-line processing of the finished die-cut sheet. Shorter runs and the ability to digitally transfer data directly to the plate, independent of location, can be expected to contribute to a wider use of this technology in flexo printing.

With the rise in printing quality, it becomes ever more important to work with the utmost care and to use material and processes that meet the requirements of reproducible, consistent printing results. It is necessary to recognize the interrelationships within the overall process in order to achieve the desired printing results faster and more easily.

Standardization Needed

In digital platemaking, the inhibiting oxygen influence during the main exposure causes the fine dots to be lower than the adjoining solids, in contrast to conventionally exposed plates using film (see *Figures 1* and *2*). Consequently, a lower printing pressure will suffice for complete reproduction of both halftones and solids. Printers refer to printing pressures close to kissprint. It

is possible to achieve homogeneous gradation of tone as well as uniform coverage in solids.

Because digitally imageable plates are lasered by different trade houses and on different laser systems, the results often differ in tonal highlight reproduction. Differing laser energies, resolutions and spot sizes greatly influence the lasering results on the plate. Additional factors are the depth of focus of the laser beam, the plate's layer structure and the absorption behavior of the black layer. In short, variations in plates, lasers and laser settings can lead to differences in tone-value transfers even before printing.

Setting up a Test File

What is needed is standardization – or at least a standardized recommendation – concerning calibration for tone-value conversion in laser imaging that takes into account the eventual printing results as measured by the printing characteristics.

Measuring the processed plates in highlight areas is either error-prone due to the few simple measuring methods available; or is ruled out because of the lack of time for more elaborate methods. Therefore, a test file should be used.

The pixel file (e.g., LEN or TIFF) should be RIP'd using the resolution of the eventual jobs. Screen rulings and anglings should also be those of the eventual jobs. The evaluation relates to the optimum test-determined processing conditions (e.g., pre-exposure, washout time). With the help of this test file, the same results should be ensured on the imaged plate, independent of the laser.

Laser Performance

Optimum laser performance should reproduce solids streak-free, without residues of the black layer. The solids laid bare by laser should have a measured optical density of ≤ 0.10. For this measuring, the densitometer is to be zeroed on a plate area bared with adhesive tape.

Fine positive and reverse elements or positive and reverse halftone dots must be reproduced in the mask at the same time. This visual check should be made on a light table (not directly in the laser), as the positive elements are hard to make out on the laser cylinder.

The effective power of an Nd:YAG laser may fluctuate due to aging or exchange of the krypton lamp. This makes it necessary to repeat the test at regular intervals. Measuring with a laser-power device can only conditionally substitute for this test of power consistency because the quality of the Nd:YAG laser output depends on its beam quality, among other factors. If simultaneous and uniform reproduction of fine positive and reverse details cannot be achieved, a laser expert should be consulted for adjustment of the laser.

In contrast, the use of a diode or fiber laser ensures constant effective output. The control software of the laser makes it possible to avoid missing spots. Nevertheless, it is still advisable to carry out the laser performance test for different plate batches.

When doing so, it is most important to know that the results relate to a specific rotational speed, a specific infeed (laser resolution) and a specific laser cylinder circumference. If any one of these three factors is changed, it is absolutely necessary to adapt the laser at the same ratio, and to carry out the performance test again.

I**f laser settings and highlight correction are treated as part of the platemaking process, tested for the different plate batches and checked at regular intervals, then the laser can be considered comparable to a film imagesetter as an output system – but at a higher level of quality regarding printing results.**

Handling Data

In data handling, consider the fact that the dots in highlight areas are two-dimensionally reduced, in diameter and in relief height (see *Figures 1* and *2*). This reduction may lead to tear-offs and missing spots and, consequently, to annoying misinterpretations on the parts of the former supplier and printer. Depending on the mentioned laser parameters – speed of rotation, rate of infeed and circumference of the laser cylinder – plus the screen ruling used, the laser data has to be corrected.

The lowest tone value of the data must be increased; i.e. it must be converted. Determining this value is done by lasering an uncorrected halftone wedge (most important being the tone value fields of 1 - 10 percent) with the laser output determined beforehand; and processing it further into a finished form.

Because of the precision of the digital technology, the subsequent conventional processing work requires particular care. Reproduction of fine elements is ensured only by exactly determining, by test, the pre-exposure and washout times and observing the recommended drying time.

Next, one must determine what tone value is anchored on the plate in a size sufficient for printing. One practical and effective solution is to inspect the plate – placed face down on a light table – with a pedestal microscope.

With the focus of the microscope adjusted to the plate-supporting surface of the light table, the dot surface should be recognizable as a distinctly defined circular area. The important thing here is that the dots must be uniform. There must be no differences (visible as a corona around the dot surface) from dot to dot in the anchoring. The lowest tone value meeting these requirements is the minimum value to which the tone should be raised in repro work or in the RIP (see *Figure 3*).

Measuring with a plate-gauging device has also proved useful. When doing so, realize that no absolute values are obtained. The systems are well suited, however, as an internal control for consistency of the plate quality achieved in processing. There is virtually no alternative to this for determining repeatable control values. The optimum would be to proof the halftone wedge (fingerprint) in order to find out what minimum tone value is the first to ensure a clean reproduction. If possible, placing the wedge in the trim margin of a job during the production run would produce the most significant information. All intermediate and final results should be documented and kept on file. The test of the highlight correction has to be repeated for every screen ruling, as the dot sizes of the different tone values differ with the screen.

In order to achieve consistent results, different plates call for different conversions, and laser performance is liable to change. Producing these characteristic tone value corrections should be done on the basis of a test-form proof, preferably under the same conditions as those of the eventual production run. This means that, for example, ink, plate support and anilox roller should largely match the parameters of the production run. In addition, it is always necessary in platemaking to take into account the different distortions caused by different laser cylinders, even with unchanged plate cylinders.

If laser settings and highlight correction are treated as part of the platemaking process, tested for the different plate batches and checked at regular intervals, then the laser can be considered comparable to a film imagesetter as an output system – but at a higher level of quality regarding printing results.

Plate Thickness

Plate thickness is another important factor. Where it is already possible to work with lower printing pressure, plates with greater thickness tolerances are liable to ruin all the potential benefits of careful digital processing. It is all the more important, therefore, to have a plate thickness with very narrow tolerances over the entire cross section.

The narrow tolerance must not only be provided by the raw plate, but ensured by the subsequent processing steps, especially wash-out and drying. Excessive differences in relief depth may influence the stability of the halftones. During drying, narrow temperature tolerances in the drying ovens must be maintained. Much more important are sufficient air circulation without dead zones in the dryer drawers, together with sufficiently long drying time.

Plate Support

The finer the screen and the thinner the plate, the more important it is to use the right support. Tonal values of 1 percent at 152 lpi, if at all useful, can be maintained only with thin plates of limited relief depth (0.020-inch - 0.025-inch). (See *Figure 4*.) This requires supports, preferably of a compressible nature, that produce high resilience and – even more critical – have pronounced true-running qualities (≤10 μm) in use on sleeves.

Any narrow tolerance in plate thickness can be made ineffective by poor-quality sleeves with bulges and high differences in wall thickness. Good-quality sleeves are an absolute necessity, as this technology is in an early stage and faced with the requirement of high register accuracy.

Check with sleeve manufacturers regarding specifics on true running. Very narrow tolerances must also be met by adhesive tape manufacturers, but taping in fine-screen areas can lead to streaks in printing.

Anilox Roller

Outstanding printing results are not guaranteed unless the digitally produced plates with screens between 137 and 152 lpi are inked with anilox rolls of sufficiently fine ruling, 60-degree angling and a fairly low pickup volume. Otherwise, the fine halftones of the plate will be drowned, resulting in prints that are irregular, cloudy and even covered with fish eyes. The target ratio should be at least 1:5 (plate:roller screens). The pickup volume (generally 2.6 - 3.5 BCM/in2) depends on type of ink, material printed and chamber doctor blade system. Consult anilox roll manufacturers.

Anyone starting out in printing from laser-imageable plates should devote extra care to the preparation of plate production and to printing. Reproducible results of consistent high quality can be achieved only by observing specific parameters and using suitable plates. Otherwise, euphoria will quickly turn into frustration. CTP is a challenge; material and knowledge are essential to success. 🐿

About the authors...
David Chinnis and Holger Neumann are with BASF Printing Systems LLC, Charlotte, NC.

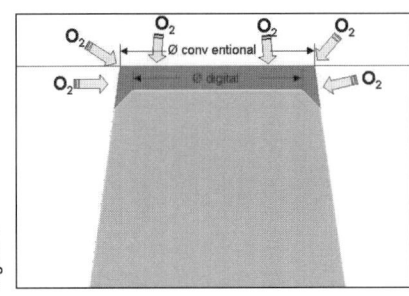

Reduction of tonal value in fine halftone screen areas based on the inhibition of oxygen

Figure 1

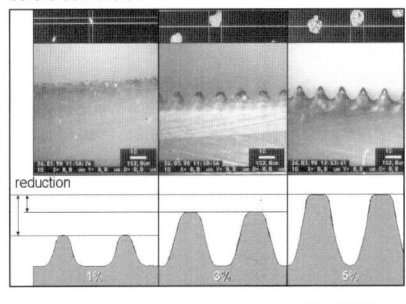

Reduction of plate thickness – tonal values of fine halftone screen dots of a 138 l/inch screen ruling before conversion

Figure 2

Microscopic verifation of fine halftone screen dots on a light table

Figure 3

In contact with glass platter

No contact with glass platter based on the reduced height of the halftone dot

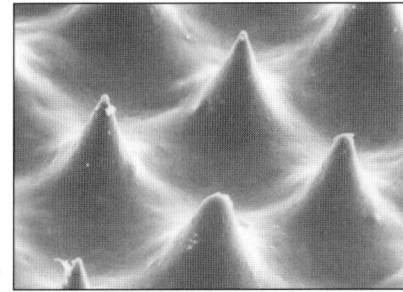

Figure 4

Example of fine halftone screen dots after digital imaging

THE FACTS ABOUT FLEXO CTP CALIBRATION AND COMPENSATION

By Tyler Harrell
Introduction by Ian Hole

FROM THE MOMENT DIGITAL FLEXO COM-puter-to-plate (CTP) imagers came on the marketplace throughout North America, it was evident that this was not just a new product, but a new technology. Tradeshops and converters embraced the idea of direct ablation of plates or sleeves, but they knew that techniques and work practices formally used to make flexo plates would have to change.

Tradeshops bought flexo digital imagers because they saw the opportunity to manage their process through calibration, control and compensation, to an extent hitherto impossible with analog plates. Converters saw the "Holy Grail" of standard settings on their presses, giving them and their end users, the consumer product companies, predictable, consistent and repeatable results, the lack of which had plagued the growth of flexography against gravure and offset for many years.

On installation of a digital imager with supporting front-end RIP, the countless tools and functionality available reveal themselves as opportunities to really control the process from package file data through customer proof to final printed package or label.

— *Ian Hole*

Calibration and Compensation

In order to understand CTP imager calibration and compensation better, definitions of these terms must be introduced.

Calibration: To standardize in such a way as to determine the validity and repeatability of a system. In the case of an imagesetter or CTP device, this must be device-dependent and process-independent. There must be validation that the device is performing to optimum specifications with consistency.

Compensation: To correct for deviation or undesirable effect. In the case of an imagesetter or CTP device, this is where process dependence is introduced. Once a device's calibration has been verified, one can then use compensation to correct for deviations from target values due to a given process.

It becomes clear that calibration is necessary to validate that a device is functioning properly and that the results can be repeated. It would be unheard of to find a device, flexo CTP included, in the field that was not and could not be calibrated! There would be no way of verifying that the equipment was in good working condition.

Traditional Methods for Calibration

From its invention by DuPont and Baasel Scheel (part of Esko-Graphics) in 1995, digital CTP ablation technology has used very traditional methods for calibration. In an imagesetter environment, calibration is based on the successful generation of a linear scale, taking into account a film's maximum and minimum density tolerances.

A flexo digital imager is calibrated with exactly the same method. Using a transmission densitometer, the ablation mask's maximum density is verified (Dmax). The ablated area is measured for stain level (Dmin). Then the linear calibration target is read to verify tonal densities.

Why Calibrate to a Linear Scale?

A linear tonal scale is used for calibration to assure that all values are equal in increment, and that they are equidistant from values immediately above and below. This maintains that there is no compression or extension of tonal values, and that therefore it is only the device that is being measured/calibrated.

Compressed or extended tonal values may affect the validity of calibration due to accuracy of the application that alters and translates the original values. It is this margin for deviation that makes a non-linear calibration philosophy unfeasible.

Natural Accuracy

In a film environment, deviations from the desired standard are typically dealt with using gamma adjustment, and in a digital imaging environment, with power adjustment. With a flexo CTP device, however, the natural output qualities are in fact quite accurate. This assures that if linear information is transmitted, it will reproduce that information with the same linear qualities. This is due to the ablative (on/off) aspect of flexo CTP, unlike a light-sensitive development environment such as film.

Outside of this aspect, the imaging phase of both

film and digital plate are similar. It is the process beyond this point where the two technologies differ greatly. What happens at this phase also has an enormous impact on the process compensation that is needed.

Built-in Compensation

In a film environment, linear output often results in plate values that are near linear and then, due to excessive dot gain, printed results that are far above target values. Additional non-linear compensation here will be beneficial to the printed result. Realize that to maintain all levels of gray, minimize highlights and maximize shadows, any method of compensation is non-linear!

In a digital flexo environment, linear output results in non-linear reduced plate values due to the absence of vacuum in the exposure process. This, combined with minimized dot gain, translates to printed values

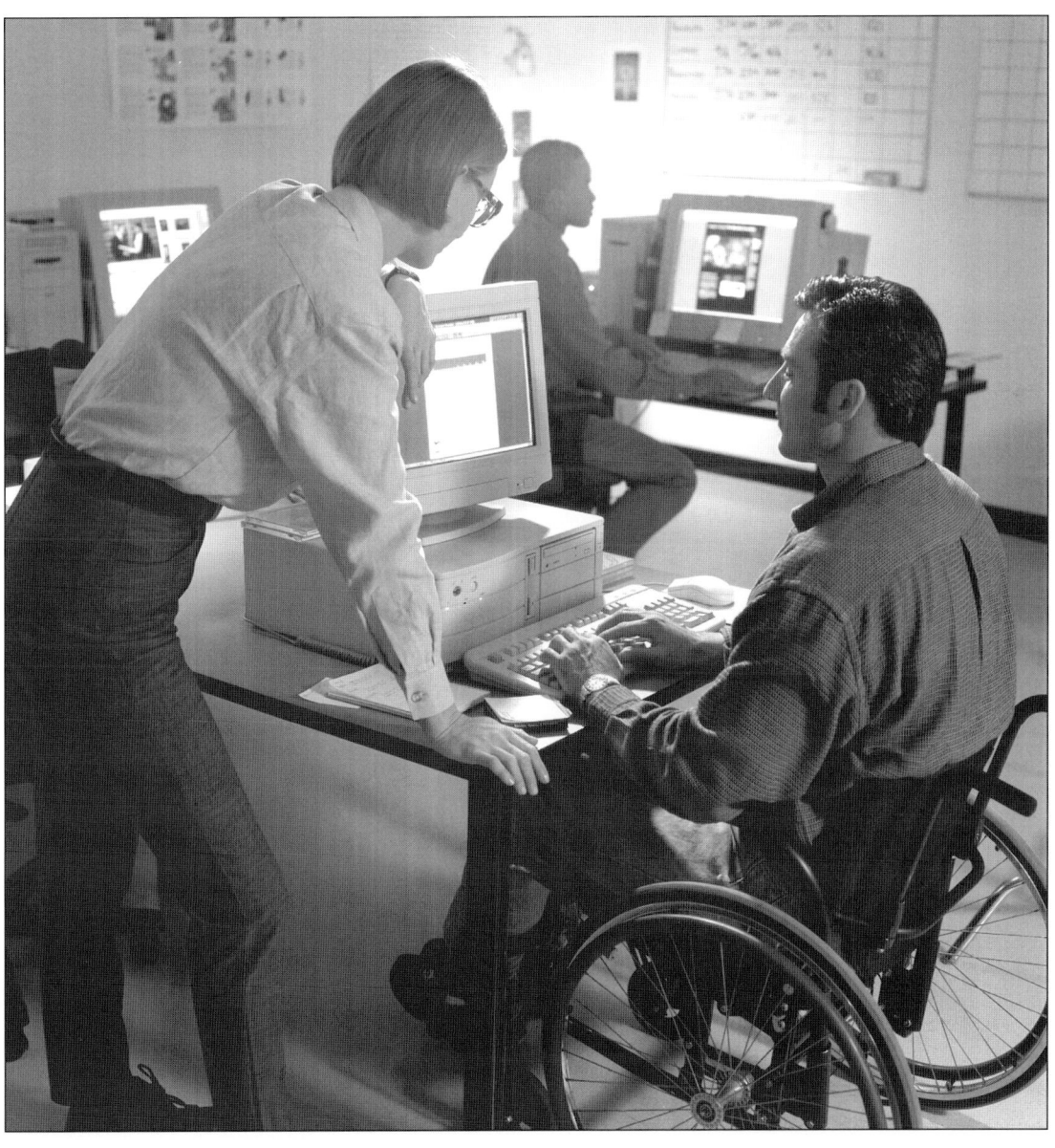

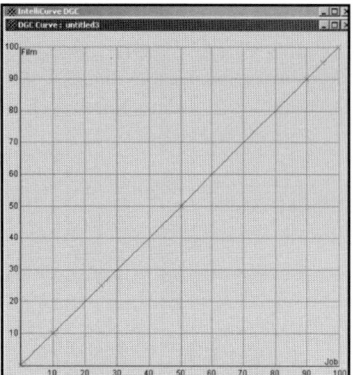

Device Calibration: A true linear scale where all values are identically progressive, and equidistant from values immediately smaller and larger. This graph illustrates the linear aspect of the digital mask.

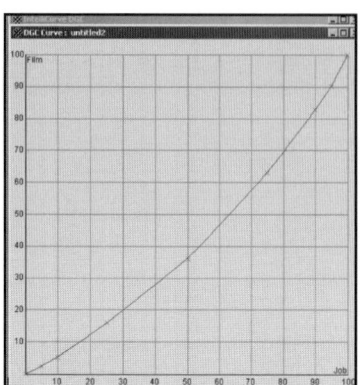

Plate Control: With the natural compensation inherent to the digital plate, the critical element is to maintain or control the natural values. The values in this graph represent the natural cutback of the finished plate.

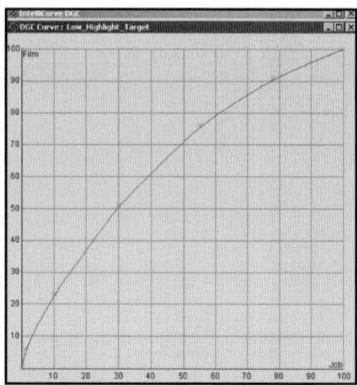

Print Compensation: Based on the deviation from target values, compensation is applied to offset any undesired results. This graph represents an example of printed values from the inherent qualities of the plate.

much closer to the target, in most cases within 7 percent of ideal values. While slight additional compensation may be beneficial, in a narrow-web environment that compensation may need to increase plate values to reduce the margin from the ideal target. Therefore, the compensation technology that is used must be flexible enough to handle both reductions and increases.

Values to Compensate For

Compensation is relative to the printed results. Therefore, alterations made to original file values must translate to enhancing the final printed tonal range. Here the plate is only a vehicle used to transport the information. This means that the imaging phase is compensated to the final printed results, not the plate values. The plate must be controlled to assure accurate and consistent translation, but again this information is only valid in how it relates to the final printed results. The plate values must, however, represent similar degrees of progression, and, again, they must be consistent.

The limitation here, of course, is the minimum printable dot that can successfully be held on the plate. Ideally, compensation performed to a file would adjust even the fine-highlight dots to offset the printed dot gain (1 percent file dot = 6 percent printed dot). It is not possible to completely counteract this trait of flexo printing. If a 1-percent dot were reduced to one-sixth its size, there would be no way to hold this on the finished plate. In digital flexo plates, a similar restriction is encountered. There is a natural reduction in dot size on a digital flexo plate caused by exposure in an oxygen environment.

Bump Curves

The crucial challenge is how to maximize the benefit of the natural non-linear compensation in the digital plate while maintaining the minimum printable dot. The solution has two parts: First the values and acceleration of the compensation curve must maintain minimum highlight values from the original file. These are generally referred to as "bump curves." These are a necessary part of any digital flexo plate workflow, and are not used in lieu of any type of calibration! In fact, they are not intended as calibration at all, but rather as compensation. The mask must be compensated for because dots that have an open area smaller than approximately .37 micron simply will not plate effectively. Remember that the CTP device was calibrated originally for linear output. Knowing this provides the confidence that any compensation performed is accurate and repeatable.

The process for determining the point at which the highlight dots fail (the crucial number for highlight compensation) must be followed precisely to avoid using a limitation that is too small or too large. Dots that are too small will not maintain printable quality, and dots too large do not maximize the benefits of the digital plate workflow.

The Formula

The instruments available for reading finished plate values have a limited capability for assisting in determining the dot-fail axis. These tools are, however, very valuable in assisting in the verification of the consistency of plate values. This is simply another validation that it is plate control, and not plate calibration or compensation, that is the goal. Remember the formula: device calibration, plate control and print compensation.

Maintaining Integrity

Once the file values have been compensated to

DIGITAL WORKFLOW Q&A

Q: Can you explain why "bump curves" are necessary in a digital plate workflow?

A: *All flexo CTP systems have limitations in the minimum open area on the ablation mask needed to maintain a printable dot. If you do not use a compensation method for maintaining this open area, you have to cut highlight values in the graphics file and consequently eliminate levels of gray. You also risk losing highlight progression and detail.*

Q: Why do I need to compensate the highlights separately for different line screens?

A: *Remember that the mini*

mum dot limitation of a flexo CTP device relates to a specific micron size. Different line screens will reach this limit at different values. A dot fail test must be implemented for all LPIs you intend to print.

Q: What about the statement that even today most flexo CTP devices remain uncalibrated?

A: *This is completely false. With more than 50 devices in North America as a testimony, if these devices were not calibrated, verification of their functionality would be impossible.*

Q: Are there really people using flexo CTP who do not incorporate print compensation curves in their workflow?

A: *Yes, absolutely! Many people find that the natural cutback curve of the plate puts them so close to the ideal target print values that any further compensation is unnecessary.*

Q: If I have a fixed form of compensation applied automatically in my workflow, and I would like to image letterpress plates or film on my CDI, will this work?

A: *It will be feasible only if this compensation is flexible enough to be altered for these other processes. If it is for flexo compensation only, then your results may suffer.*

— Tyler Harrell

accommodate the digital imaging workflow, the second part of the compensation process must maintain the integrity of this compensation, and work in conjunction with it to provide optimum results on press.

Technologies that only provide for a single compensation will, in many cases, require excessive trial and error, and may even then not achieve ideal results. The most effective method for realizing ideal results is to have the opportunity to apply two separate compensation curves.

The curve that is applied for maintaining highlights is fixed and depends only on variance in line screen ruling. This should be applied in a background mode and not be user-dependant. It assures that the minimum dot will always be maintained. When creating a compensation curve or using a pre-defined generic curve, it is also beneficial to visualize the interaction between the two compensations.

The biggest danger in compensation in a flexo CTP workflow is to flatten or actually invert highlight and quarter tone values. This will cause defects in the visual aspect of the printed piece. Unfortunately, many automatic compensation technologies provide entirely too large a margin for this error, and many user-interactive technolo-

gies do not have the internal sophistication to provide a smooth progression of values for either the highlight compensation or the print compensation. There are technologies available that will provide the accuracy and integrity needed, and a simple characterization test will make the determination as to which of these is appropriate for a given workflow.

Conclusions

Flexo digital imaging is by far the most consistent and controlled technology available to the industry today. It provides severe reductions in dot gain, and by nature incorporates its own almost ideal non-linear print compensation. It is, however, the overall integrity of the workflow and the applications that account for the difference between improved results and exceptional results.

The philosophy of device calibration, plate control and print compensation, along with a workflow system that acknowledges this, will provide ultimate success!

About the authors...
Ian Hole is business development manager for Esko-Graphics, Vandalia, OH. Tyler Harrell is manager of Esko-Graphics' FIQ (Flexo Implementation Quality), a program to help customers through the technology learning curve and into the world of digital control and all its advantages.

Prepress for Envelopes
Extra Care at Each Step Yields Customer-Pleasing Results

By Reid Andereson

When one thinks of digital prepress, one envisions technicians imposing pages and dovetailing or nesting graphics that would fulfill prepress needs common to many printing applications. But with envelopes, a different mindset is required. Envelope presses print, cut out the sides, score, cut and patch a window, glue, fold and add seal gum at speeds of up to 1,000 envelopes per minute. Narrow-web printing is done on very small cylinders at high speeds. Proper plate relief and sticky back with proper kiss impression is crucial for both high-quality printing and attaining any measurable plate life.

The prepress department staff must be in tune not only with flexography, but also with how it relates to the envelope and the envelope equipment it is to be manufactured with. There are many styles of envelopes. The prepress shop must know each of these envelope styles and how they're to be manufactured:

- The booklet style (commonly referred to as double side seam) has its opening on the larger dimension. This has become the most popular envelope in direct mail because of its insertability.

- The open-end envelope has its opening on the shorter dimension and usually has a center seam on the back; however, there are several side-seam styles in use.

- The bangtail has a perforated coupon attached to the body of a return envelope that must be torn off before the envelope can be sealed. This is used mainly for remittance envelopes, order envelopes and other direct mail applications.

- The diagonal-seam envelope is used mainly for invitations or announcements.

Whereas commercial sheet-fed and web printers refer to sheet size and repeat, respectively, envelope manufacturers/printers refer to repeat or blank size;

i.e., the size of the unfolded blank before it enters the folding sections. When speaking of commercial envelopes, the height is stated first, then the width. For example, a 6-inch by 9-inch envelope is 6 inches high by 9 inches wide.

Windows are also an important part of prepress. Customers need to see proofs of the envelope with window size and position indicated. Windows are specified by their width and length. The length is the horizontal measurement and the width is the height of the window. Positioning of the window is critical; it is measured from the left and bottom side of the envelope with the flap on top.

Prepress Procedures

An envelope order typically states the envelope size, style, flap size and style, window size and position (if there is a window), number of colors and the press it is scheduled to be printed on. Hopefully, native files have been supplied with a hard copy for a visual. It is necessary to pre-flight the files before doing any other work. If the file or any support files are missing, are corrupt, have the incorrect resolutions or are otherwise unusable, prepress work cannot begin.

A template or outline of the exact envelope being produced is critical if there are bleeds and/or printing is to be done on the back or the flap of the envelope. Typically, these templates are drawn in vector format (.eps) in an application such as Adobe Illustrator or the equivalent. Once the template is drawn, the artwork can begin to be merged with the template.

First, the template is brought into the customer-supplied files. This insures that all copy stays where it should, preferences are retained and there are no surprises. It is best to have the document size roughly two inches larger than the template. This allows for a one-inch clearance all around.

If a window is required, this is the time to indicate its size and placement in the file. Remember, the window placement is measured from left and bottom of the face of the envelope with the flap on top. If

The customer's expectations are high. It is up to the prepress people to do their homework to alert everyone concerned of any potential printing issues that may arise. **99**

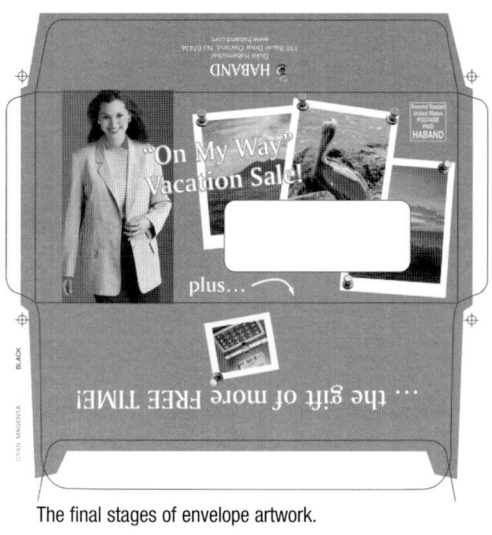

The final stages of envelope artwork.

the flap is on the side of the envelope, the window must still be positioned with the flap on the top. Don't get too confused here. Just remember that the window is always measured with the flap on top regardless of how the envelope will be used. If the order requires a window on the back, it will still be positioned using measurements from the left score and bottom fold.

Bleed Rules

If the artwork calls for full bleeds, there are some rules to follow. The majority of envelopes produced are booklet-style envelopes, with the bleed off the flap typically 1/16-inch to 3/32-inch. The back is where the plate is gapped for the full wrap of the printing cylinder. This is done under the flap to hide the substrate color and allow for a good "gum line," which is used when sealing the envelope. Normally the side-seam bleeds can run halfway into the seams. This is where the exact template of the final piece is critical. The taper of the back coupled with the taper of the flap determines the bleed into the side seams. If the envelope is relatively square, usually there are no problems. However, if the tapers are severe, the bleeds may have to be extended and angled to hide the substrate. The best check is to print a paper proof and cut and fold it into the envelope. This is an example of how to think ahead when working on future artwork.

Envelope folding equipment typically has a 1/16-inch variance. The envelope blank does not have the luxury of having a gripper or side guide. It is transferred from cylinder to cylinder through the folding process with vacuum

power; thus, the slight movement and variance. The United States Postal Service (and other worldwide posts) realizes this, and their automated equipment is designed to work within these tolerances.

It is important to allow for this variance on the artwork if there are any graphics or colors that are supposed to butt up to the top or bottom folds. Artwork that butts exactly to the folds will vary through folding, and the back or flap color or graphics will spill over to the face of the envelope and vice versa – something the customer probably doesn't want to see.

Color Trapping

Spot color inks are neither opaque nor transparent, so one must be careful when overprinting or having large overlaps of different colors. Colors need to have slight overlaps to correct for misregistration on the press. The overlaps should not be too large or too small. A trap of from 1/2 to 1 point (.007-.014) gives minimal overlap and presents the best chance for the press operators to achieve

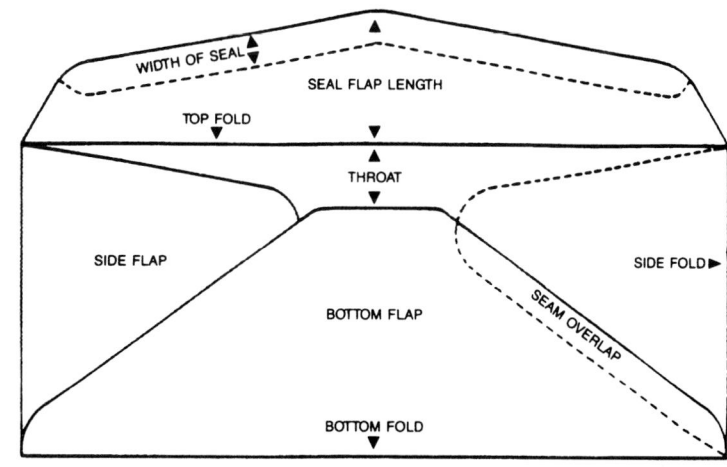

The anatomy of an envelope.

desired results. What is overprinted depends on the colors, the size of the object vs. background, etc. There are no hard and fast rules.

RIP-based trapping solutions provide adequate trapping roughly 60 percent of the time. Manual trapping in the native files is still held in high regard. Informing the customer of potential problems due to the design is always important. Depending on the design, it might be necessary to overprint an object color in some areas and trap it in others. This may give the appearance of two different shades of a color that was designed to be one.

Color & Ink Concerns

Generally, envelopes are printed on an uncoated, commodity-grade, very absorbent paper, in most cases with water-based inks. When these inks are printed on this paper, drying is achieved by approximately 80 percent absorption and 20 percent evaporation. This has a tendency to cause substantial dot gain. Cutback (dot gain compensation) is critical to reproducing the artwork in the way it was designed.

Some ink coverage concerns center around whether we are trying to print large solids and screens of the same color, and whether we have the option of breaking out colors and printing them on multiple units. Are we trying to print small fine serifs that may be too hard to hold? How about rule weights? All of these issues need to be addressed. We want the artwork to be as flexo-friendly as possible without compromising the original design.

Many times designers do not check their color

Flexographic envelope printing on the web.

assignments or naming conventions. There must be consistent color assignments so the artwork will separate as intended. Watch out for Pantone colors that are the same, but are named differently. Printing separations to a black-and-white printer provides a quick check. Is the artwork separating as needed? If not, alterations are required to correct the problem.

Know Your Press

Knowing the character of the presses to be used allows prepress technicians to provide proper cutback in screened areas for dot gain. There is usually substantial dot gain, but it differs from press to press. Prepress needs to make recommendations to sales and customer service personnel if there are concerns.

Using double or triple spot color knockouts as a design solution is also dependent on the press being printed on. A CI press that has excellent registration and a stack press where the registration is not as tight may require different trapping techniques to achieve desirable results.

How well the original design is reproduced is very important. The customer's expectations are high. It is up to the prepress people to do their homework to alert everyone concerned of any potential printing issues that may arise. Prepress plays a vital role in the quality of the final printed piece.

About the Author...
Reid Anderson is prepress manager for Mackay Envelope Corp., Minneapolis, MN.

Flexible Packaging
Maximizes Shelf Appeal & Brand Awareness

Photo courtesy of Avery Dennison

By Chris Mitchell

Years ago, when consumers were offered coffee "choices," they were presented with a selection of ground, decaf, instant or whole bean. Then coffee manufacturers started to differentiate their products by introducing new blends and flavors – French vanilla, French roast, hazelnut and classic supreme. Today, in the quest for increased market share, companies are mass marketing those products once considered specialties, such as café latte. Consumers are drinking it up, but the manufacturers' thirst for market differentiation still isn't satisfied.

Take a walk down the store aisle and look at how coffee manufacturers are presenting their products these days. You'll find coffee cans wrapped in flexible packaging, vacuum-sealed packages, resealable stand-alone flexible packages, folding carton boxes with individual coffee singles and full-body shrink packaging. It is not unusual for one brand to take up to six feet of top-to-bottom shelf space due to the variety of flavors and packaging offered to the consumer.

Flexible packaging often proves an ideal solution for manufacturers who want to maximize shelf appeal and increase brand awareness. Used by nearly every industry, flexible packaging protects and preserves products, as well as meets the growing need for innovative packaging design. Moreover, flexible packaging offers consumers what they most desire: speed and convenience.

For these and many other reasons, flexible packaging opportunities continue to evolve. Printers have

Flexible packaging often proves
an ideal solution
for manufacturers who want
to maximize shelf appeal
and increase brand awareness.
Used by nearly every industry,
flexible packaging protects
and preserves products,
as well as
meets the growing need
for innovative
packaging design.

the opportunity to distinguish themselves and to build substantial growth for their businesses by fulfilling this growing need. This article covers the exact

nature of flexible packaging and the many new business opportunities it presents, as well as how to access the best resources and ensure long- and short-term customer satisfaction.

Multi-Layered Structures

Generally taking the shape of bags, pouches, roll labels, liners or wraps, flexible packaging has no form of its own but conforms to the product contained within. Its pliable, non-rigid properties use paper, plastic film, aluminum foil or a combination of these products to create a multi-layer structure that in some cases rivals rigid packaging.

Flexible packages are multi-layered structures available in paper- and film-faced laminated pouch materials. The structure can include layers providing barrier properties, stiffness and flexibility, strength, aesthetics and sealant properties. The composition and thickness of each layer is designed to provide specific performance characteristics in the finished film.

An exterior layer serves as the outside of a multi-layered structure. This layer can provide printability, dimension stability, heat resistance, stiffness/flexibility, flex crack resistance, low co-efficient of friction (COF), clarity, aesthetics and tear resistance and/or propagation. Materials commonly used in the exterior layer are biaxially oriented polypropylene (BOPP), biaxially oriented polyester (OPET), biaxially oriented nylon (BON), paper and cast nylon. BOPP, OPET, BON and paper are frequently printed. Cast nylon is often coated onto the surface of barrier or sealant films because it can be molded into a desired shape under heat and vacuum.

A barrier layer is added to the multi-layered structure for protection. In this layer, barrier properties against oxygen, light, moisture and odor – along with chemical resistance and bond strength – are provided. The property requirements will vary depending on the product being packaged, the desired shelf life and the packaging, storage and distribution conditions of the finished product. Typical barrier materials used are polyvinyledene dichloride (PVdC), silicone dioxide (SiOx), ethylene vinyl alcohol (EVOH), aluminum foil and metallized (met) films.

The most common clear barrier materials are PVdC, SiOx and EVOH. PVdC and SiOx are used in coated and laminated films, while EVOH is used in co-extruded blown sealants and films. Aluminum foil offers an excellent moisture and oxygen barrier, but cannot be used in thermoforming applications. Metallized barrier products include met OPET, met OPP and met BON. Met OPET is often used in coffee packaging. It is less expensive than foil, offering an excellent oxygen barrier. It also provides good heat resistance when used as an exterior mate-

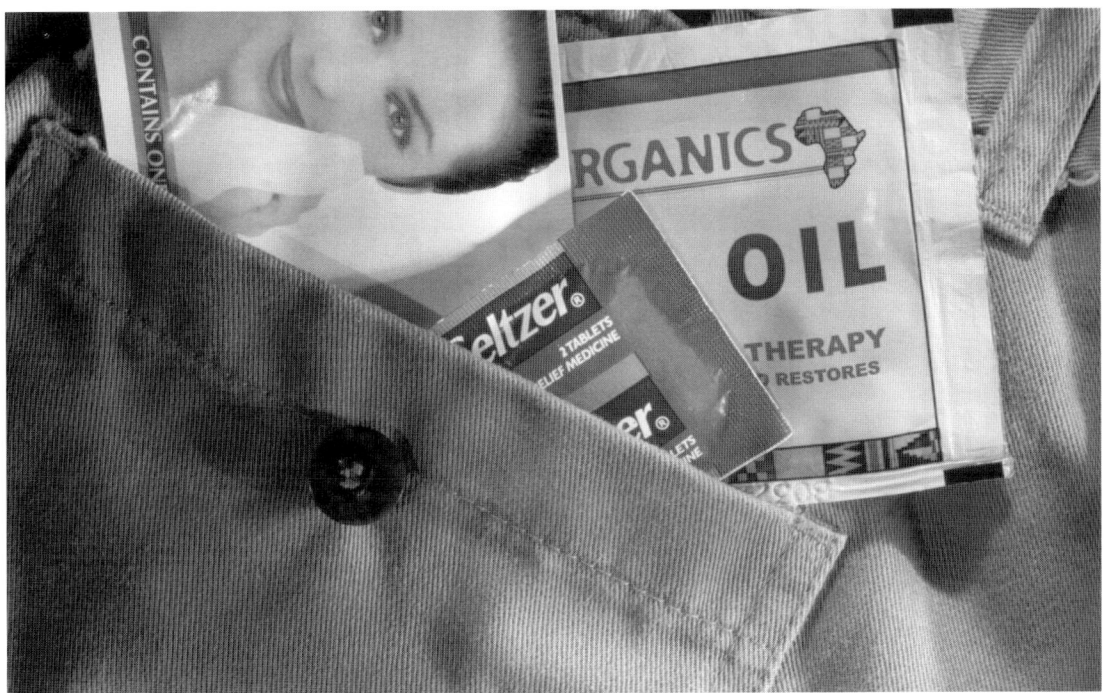

Photo courtesy of Avery Dennison

rial. Met OPP provides good moisture barrier and is used for snack films, as they do not require as much oxygen barrier. Finally, met BON is used in bulk coffee packaging where strength is essential.

Sealant material will adhere to itself or to another film when heat and pressure are applied to produce hermetic seals. This prevents gases from penetrating through the seals into the package. Typically applied to the inside layer of a multi-layer structure, the performance characteristics vary depending on the product being packaged and the type and speed of the packaging machinery. The most common materials used are low-density polyethylene (LDPE), ultra-linear low-density polyethylene (ULLDPE), linear-low-density polyethylene (LLDPE), polyethylene-vinyl acetate (EVA), Surlyn, polyethylene acrylic acid (EAA), polyethylene methacrylic acid (EMAA) and metallocene linear-low-density polyethylene (m-LLDPE).

In general, sealants that contain LDPE, ULLDPE and LLDPE tend to be lower in cost. Surlyn is often used in meat packaging, as it seals well through contamination and grease. EAA and EMAA sealants form tight chemical bonds and are often used to protect metal-containing films from high-acid foods, as well as hard-to-hold products like sunscreens and fruit oils. Finally, m-LLDPE is clearer, has lower seal initiation temperature and better hot tack properties than LLDPE, but does not seal as well through contamination.

Narrow-Web Advantage

The rise in innovative flexible packaging creates enormous opportunities for printers. This is especially true for narrow-web printers who generally convert product less than 26 inches. Noted for taking on smaller order sizes and turning around product quickly, these operations almost always have reduced plate and press costs and more flexibility than their wide-web counterparts.

The demand for greater variety and innovations with private-label brands is growing, as consumers tend to be less loyal to national brands. This, in combination with the drive for handy take-and-go products, creates a natural fit for a narrow-web printer, as a quick review of overall opportunities in flexible packaging reveals.

- Narrow-web presses are ideal for new product roll outs, when a manufacturer may want to test or launch a product in smaller markets or a number of regions before investing in a nationwide promotion.

- Running product samples for direct-mail campaigns becomes big business for a narrow-web printer. These small packets, eventually containing wipes, lotions or shampoos, are a perfect fit for small runs.

- Both primary and secondary pouches provide printing opportunities. Primary packaging has four purposes: to contain, protect, promote and communicate. This type of packaging requires aesthetically pleasing packages that are also functional. Many possibilities are available in non-retail markets – also known as secondary packaging – for dry soups, spices, non-dairy creamers, cocoa mixes and pharmaceutical applications.

- Roll-fed glue-applied film labels have exploded due

to better durability and more natural ink snap than paper alternatives. Rising interest in health and exercise has grown the demand for energy drinks, sport drinks and bottled waters, increasing opportunities for small order sizes.

- Shrink sleeve films are giving products a bold, full-body look, 360-degree graphics and built-in tamper evidence capabilities. New-age beverages, juice/ yogurt drinks and single-serve flavored milks are making an impression in the marketplace. Both roll-fed glue-applied film labels and shrink-sleeve film applications allow manufacturers to inventory one can type or can size. Manufacturers no longer need to preprint cans, reducing their inventory and waste costs. By using roll stock, very little change-over is necessary when a manufacturer needs to transition to different product brands or offer chocolate instead of vanilla flavoring.

- Wide-web converters are aligning themselves with companies that have narrow-web capabilities, utilizing the partnership as a second source or in capacity situations. Typically, they work with major clients that require large orders, but periodically have small orders that can be run more efficiently at a narrow-web house.

form best on the latest equipment. More ink suppliers are offering a broad range of choices specifically designed for flexible packaging products, as well.

Selecting the Right Product

Common flexible packaging products for narrow-web applications include polyester (PET), LDPE, Paper Poly Foil Poly (PPFP), Paper Poly Metallized Polypropylene (PPMOPP), BOPP/OPP and film-laminated products. These multi-layered structures are designed to meet the needs of today's most in-demand applications: packaging that is portable, easy to open and resealable for busy consumers, as well as lighter and easier to inventory and transport for manufacturers.

While cost, appearance and performance are driving manufacturers to choose flexible packaging in general, it is important for printers to understand how each application will be used in order to ensure ultimate customer satisfaction. Will the package be used for dry goods or liquids? Does it require heat resistance, stability or strength? Must it conceal an aroma? Does it need to provide a protective security barrier? The answers to these questions will determine the appropriate product in the short term and gain market share and build a strong customer base in the long run.

As Steve Grace, president of Grace Label, comments,

Flexible packaging opportunities continue to evolve. Printers have the opportunity to distinguish themselves and to build substantial growth for their businesses by fulfilling this growing need.

Education and Technical Support

A growing number of narrow-web converters are beginning to focus their efforts on packaging opportunities. While printers are very familiar with running tag and label applications, flexible packaging adds a few twists to the learning curve. Some of the challenges are sales- and marketing-focused, but others are press-related and have to do with changes in web tensioning, heat dispersion and ink adhesion with films.

Manufacturing experience can overcome the learning curve. Many times, especially when running paper-faced laminated pouch products, printers may simply need to make adjustments to their existing equipment. Lightweight films requiring low web tension and low processing temperatures are prime examples of new, specialty applications that may per-

"We found that converting the product was easy. The most challenging part of the process is specifying the correct material for the application and then acquiring the product from a supplier in a timely manner. Lead times directly from a manufacturer can easily be five to six weeks or more. You need to develop a relationship with a supplier that has product knowledge and can readily supply you."

Ready Resources

There are a host of ready-made resources available to the printer thinking of expanding flexible packaging operations. Whether the end use is for a food product, pharmaceutical, health/beauty, chemical or fertilizer application, suppliers have the depth of experience and resources to complement existing in-house expertise.

Similarly, a contract packager can fill, secure and ship the finished package if you are asked to finish the package. Contract packagers can usually be found locally, offering a variety of services designed for F/F/S (form/fill/seal) applications. Most will have in-house horizontal, vertical and pouch packaging capabilities, plus offer fulfillment, warehousing and distribution services.

Flexible packaging continues to evolve and applications increase as new materials, including shrink products, are being introduced. Pay attention to how products are packaged and look for new sources of business. Remember the last time you used the coffee maker in your hotel room? It was stashed with packages of coffee, cream and sugar, all bundled in easy-to-open flexible packaging.

Manufacturers will continue to look for new ways to market and differentiate their products. With a relatively small learning curve and a wealth of outside resources, printers are poised to fulfill the growing needs for innovative and diverse flexible packaging solutions.

About the Author...
Chris Mitchell is Fasson® Rapid-Roll® flexible packaging product manager at Avery Dennison, Neenah, WI. Mitchell provides Fasson-brand flexible packaging products in roll form, along with experience and technical support to flexible packaging customers in the narrow-web industry. Mitchell, who has been working in the field for more than 15 years, holds a bachelor of business administration degree in finance from the University of Wisconsin – Oshkosh.

Paper-Making Procedures
Substrate Improvements Advance the Envelope Industry

By Kathy Collins

Feeling flexo-challenged? The flexographic printing of envelopes is one of the fastest growing segments in the printing industry, with annual percentage growth figures in the double digits. This growth is due in large part to the fact that improvements in flexographic printing of paper have brought it to a level that its appearance is often competitive with offset printing. Other factors include the expanding direct mail market and the relatively low cost of manufacturing flexo printed envelopes.

Historically, most envelopes have been printed using an offset press. The configuration of the offset press requires multiple and distinct processes to be completed in order to produce a finished envelope. For example: The roll of paper is sheeted, the sheets are printed and stacked, the stacks are die cut and the die-cut blanks are converted in a machine that performs the folding and sealing operations. The cost-savings aspect of using flexography versus offset for envelopes is derived from reduction in turnaround time and paper waste.

The configuration of the flexographic press enables the individual steps to be consolidated into one in-line process, beginning with a roll of paper and ending with a printed envelope. Elimination of the intermediate sheeting and stack die-cutting steps dramatically reduces the amount of paper waste generated. Past figures indicate that a ratio of 70 percent of envelopes were printed offset versus just 30 percent flexo for the four-color and six-color markets. Trends indicate that these numbers will actually reverse over the next few years.

What Is Paper?

In the simplest of terms, paper is essentially a dried blend of wood fiber, water and filler that sometimes has a coating applied to the surface. The papermaking process begins as the fiber/water/filler mixture (98 percent water at this point) is deposited onto a moving wire screen. Water begins to drain through the wire, and the movement of the wire helps set the grain direction and "formation" of the paper. The web is then transported via a fabric felt through high-pressure nips where it is compressed and more water is removed. Paper passes through dryers that reduce the water content to less than 5 percent. At this point, a coat of starch-based sizing is usually applied, then the sheet is re-dried. An on-line coating may be applied at this time as well; however, many times the coating is instead applied in a separate process using an off-line coater.

The last step in the papermaking process is the calender section. This is the point at which the sheet is made smoother and a consistent caliper is ensured across the web. The finished web is wound into a large reel (for some newer machines, sizes range upwards of 350 inches across the web), which is subsequently slit into smaller rolls according to the product needs.

Paper Properties

In the past, the primary characteristics that were targeted in flexo envelope papers were strength and convertibility. In the evolving world of flexographically printed envelopes, both strength and a highly printable surface are important. This section details some of the properties that are important in making a high-

Envelope substrate set up on the rewinder section of the press.

quality envelope paper. For superior print performance, some of the characteristics to look for include:

- **Smoothness:** A smooth surface will allow good ink coverage with low ink film thickness using components that yield minimal dot gain.

- **Uniformity:** Caliper, formation (distribution of components) and moisture should be as uniform as possible across the web for a high-quality printing sheet.

- **Ink Hold-Out:** When paper has good ink hold-out, more pigment remains on the surface of the paper, resulting in better ink density and giving more "snap" to the appearance. While various properties affect ink hold-out, porosity (air permeability) is one of the more important characteristics.

- **Wettability/Ink Absorption:** The paper should allow quick drying of the ink. This will minimize any tracking of ink, especially on presses that are not equipped with dryers. Ultimately, the most important aspect of paper to a flexographic printer, no matter what type of paper substrate chosen, is consistency: across the web, throughout the roll, between rolls and between lots. In particular, consistent caliper and surface smoothness are critical because of the sensitivity of the "kiss" impression with flexographic printing. Advances in paper machine technology have had a significant impact on the paper industry's ability to control sheet consistency and uniformity, thus equipping the newest paper machines with the tools needed to surpass standards set by many conventional machines in operation today.

No matter how nicely a sheet prints, it must also convert well to be a successful envelope paper. If converting the paper results in multiple

Fiber: Wood fiber, usually a mix of hardwood and soft wood. This gives the sheet its strength and bulk properties.

Filler: Chemical additives such as calcium carbonate and titanium dioxide that enhance the opacity, brightness and smoothness of the paper.

Sizing: A starch-based coating that seals the surface of the paper, improving resistance to fiber or filler being pulled from the sheet.

Coating: Usually clay-based with a binder such as latex or starch and other additives. The absence of fiber on the surface, along with the properties of the coating components, allows a super-smooth, sometimes glossy finish to be achieved.

jams and increased downtime, the savings of flexographic printing can be lost through reduced efficiency and wasted raw materials. Properties important to successful converting include:

- **Stiffness:** If the paper does not have sufficient stiffness, it may tend to fold incorrectly or may jam in the envelope equipment.

- **Lack of Curl:** Because of the nature of wood fibers, paper often has a tendency to curl when exposed to changes in temperature or humidity. It is important to counteract this tendency in order to avoid jamming in the converting equipment.

- **Moisture Content:** Moisture content should be at an optimum level and be consistent throughout the sheet. Moisture that is too low may result in cracks appearing at the folds, while moisture that is too high may result in higher curl tendencies.

- **Fiber Orientation:** Control of the average fiber direction aids in maintaining good curl resistance and dimensional stability.

In addition to good convertibility at the envelope plant, trouble-free performance during the inserting process is also critical. Some of the properties that impact this performance include:

- **Porosity:** Some facilities utilize vacuum feed insertion systems. Paper that is too porous will not perform well in this equipment.

- **Strength at the Fold:** Good overall strength properties ensure that the fold will not rupture when materials are inserted.

- **Stiffness:** This property is important for successful insertion as well as for converting.

- **Brightness/Shade:** While brightness and shade can impact the appearance of a spot-printed envelope, many times this property is important only from a visual perspective. The marketing value of this needs to be determined by the end user and the converter.

- **Basis Weight:** Envelope papers are generally sold in lbs. (signified by #) of 500 17-inch by 22-inch sheets. Common weights are 20#, 24#, and 28#. In contrast, offset printing grades (non-envelope papers) are usually sold as 500 lbs. of 25-inch by 38-inch sheets. A conversion factor of 2.54 can be used to translate one into the other. For example, a 20# envelope paper is comparable in weight to a 50.8# offset paper.

Paper Substrates

There are three primary types of papers available for flexo-printed envelopes: uncoated wove, premium uncoated/lightly coated and fully coated. (The scope of this article is limited to white papers used for printing. There are a variety of other envelope substrates such as kraft-colored and cushion-lined. These markets are much smaller and don't generally involve much, if any, printing).

Uncoated Wove: The wove substrates are the "workhorse" of envelope papers. Their appealing attributes are strength and relatively low cost. They are bulky; have good stiffness and body; and convert and insert very well at high speeds. Uncoated woves, however, are not designed or optimized for printing high-end process jobs. With its rougher surface, a wove substrate is not as good for printing fine screens using a thin ink film. With the increase in flexographic printing for envelopes, paper suppliers are working to optimize the printability of these envelope papers without compromising convertibility. Wove papers are most commonly utilized in 20# or 24# weights. While each plant's capabilities are different, you might see a wove paper being used for jobs with spot color (mostly text and solids), or halftones in the range of 85 lpi–100 lpi.

Premium Uncoated/ Lightly Coated: These envelope papers are fairly new to the market. They have evolved in response to the need for an affordable sheet that can be printed with four-color to eight-color demanding graphics for which a wove sheet might not be suitable. In order to fulfill these requirements, paper in this category will typically have a much smoother surface than a wove sheet, but still retain good stiffness and body for trouble-free converting. The smooth surface that these papers offer allows a thinner ink film to be used while maintaining a "kiss" impression for minimal dot gain. Many times these grades are chosen for four-color process jobs with plate line screens above 100. While this is an evolving group of papers, they are usually available in heavier weights (more than 24#).

Fully Coated: Fully coated envelope papers may be offered with coating on one or both sides. Because of the envelope application, however, a coated-one-side (C1S) is most often seen. The coating is typically clay-based. This enables a gloss, or shininess, to be achieved on the surface of the sheet if desired. The coating also provides good ink hold-out. The gloss and ink hold-out result in printing that has a certain "snap" to its appearance. Coated sheets also have the smoothest surfaces of envelope paper substrates, allowing a finer plate screen (133+) to be used with a thin ink film and reduced dot gain. Coated papers, however, are generally the highest in cost. They are mostly offered in 28# weights. This is likely due to two factors:

ORDERING PAPER

Placing an order for paper that will be used in a flexo envelope operation is pretty straightforward. Because these machines are web-fed, one simply has to specify to the paper manufacturer the roll properties needed. Envelopes are generally oriented parallel to the machine direction of the paper, so the width of the roll should be equal to the width of the envelope blank (allowing for the side folds). Be sure to specify the appropriate core size required for your equipment and the maximum outside diameter of the roll that can be handled.

The cost-savings aspect of using flexography versus offset for envelopes is derived from reduction in turn-around time and paper waste.

- Due to the higher cost, coated papers are more likely to be used in high-end jobs where it is desirable to have a sheet with a smooth yet "substantial" feel to it.

- Because the coating takes up space that strength-giving fibers would otherwise occupy, a higher weight is necessary to achieve good stiffness for converting, although the yield of envelopes per pound of paper is sacrificed in this process.

In addition to the envelope grades available, many printers choose to use other paper grades not specifically designed for envelopes. While these may have surfaces that can be printed well, the user should be aware that the paper was most likely built for a less demanding converting operation. These papers may not always have the same stiffness, or body, that corresponding envelope grades do, and more difficulties in the folding equipment could result.

Selecting a Substrate

The two primary considerations in selecting an appropriate envelope substrate are the print requirements of the job and the expected selling price of the envelope. For example, if the job you want to print is a four-color process job with printing more than 90 percent of the envelope and plate screens above 100 lpi, you may want to consider either a premium uncoated or a coated stock. On the other hand, if the job is less than 50 percent print coverage with a lot of

text and solids, you could probably achieve good quality print with a less expensive wove substrate. Your customer may also have a preference and may dictate or influence the paper chosen. Another concern may be drying capabilities. If you would like to use a coated stock, be sure that the ink system you are using and the press drying capabilities are suitable for use on coated papers.

One important thing to keep in mind is that every press is different, and the substrate is only one of several variables that will impact the print quality. The combination of choices made for plate material, plate screen, stickyback, ink and anilox cell volume as well as substrate will ultimately dictate the appearance of the final print. The best action a printer can take is to conduct tests using several combinations of components to determine the result of various substrates under different conditions. One convenient testing tool is the banded anilox. A reference book can be maintained of the different set-ups with examples of each. When the time comes to decide on a substrate for a new job, the printer can refer to this book to identify the components needed to achieve the desired result.

The world of flexographic envelopes is an exciting place to be right now. Having a basic understanding of paper characteristics and their potential impact on print quality and converting speed can help the converter obtain the right substrate for a particular job. In fact, balancing the capabilities of the press and the capabilities of the substrate is critical to success. Spending a little time up front studying each component of the process should ultimately pay big dividends down the road. 🎇

About the Author...
Kathy Collins is a development engineer at Willamette Industries' East Coast Development Lab in Fort Mill, SC. Willamette, a Weyerhaeuser subsidiary, manufactures several different paper grades, including two types of envelope papers, wove and premium uncoated (ci2000).

QUICK-CHANGE TECHNOLOGY

PROPER PRESSROOM PRACTICES YIELD OPTIMUM RESULTS

By Ed Dedman

One of the biggest challenges facing any print operation today is the task of reducing job setup and changeover times in the pressroom. The pressure to increase productivity and, correspondingly, profit continues to grow on a daily basis. To achieve this increased productivity, many print operations are turning to presses equipped with technologies designed to enhance and improve job change functions through a variety of means. Most of the commonly used technologies offer some variation on the "print cartridge" concept, wherein the components of the actual print unit are assembled into a movable/removable assembly. These variations include, but are not limited to, the following:

- Slide-out inking drawers, with quick-release anilox and plate cylinder attachments

- Movable inking and/or print cassettes

- Cassettes with ancillary equipment such as ransport carts, cleaning stations, etc.

- Interchangeable print cassette/print method systems
  Some of the chief advantages offered by these systems are minimization of press downtime due to job setup, which makes for more available production time; faster turnaround times on jobs, a competitive advantage; less manual handling of expensive press components and lower costs associated with anilox damage and blade injuries.

All of these technologies have advantages and disad-

The Pressroom Supply Web

vantages, but they all have one thing in common: They are dependent upon all other variables in the pressroom being correct in order to achieve their full functionality and benefit.

In the following paragraphs, we'll revisit the basics in order to assure that all pressroom variables are accounted for and minimized, to realize an optimum level of job-change efficiency. While most of these variables are commonly recognized, many print shops don't regularly control them.

Beginning with job ticket, let's look at how the "supply chain" concept can be utilized internally, becoming an actual "supply web," and identify the co-relationships among the different components of this "web."

Job Ticket

Most shops use some type of job ticket/jacket/card in order to provide basic information to the press crew. This basic information should include, at the very least, information on the customer, a description of the run specifications, the quantity in feet or pieces, any special requirements and the ship date needed. With this information as an absolute minimum, the job ticket should also include specifications for anilox, substrate, ink, plates, mounting tape and dies.

Once this information is available on this job ticket, it is imperative that all parties involved READ and FOLLOW this information. The No. 1 reason that most repeat jobs don't match the previous run is that one or more of these variables is different than before.

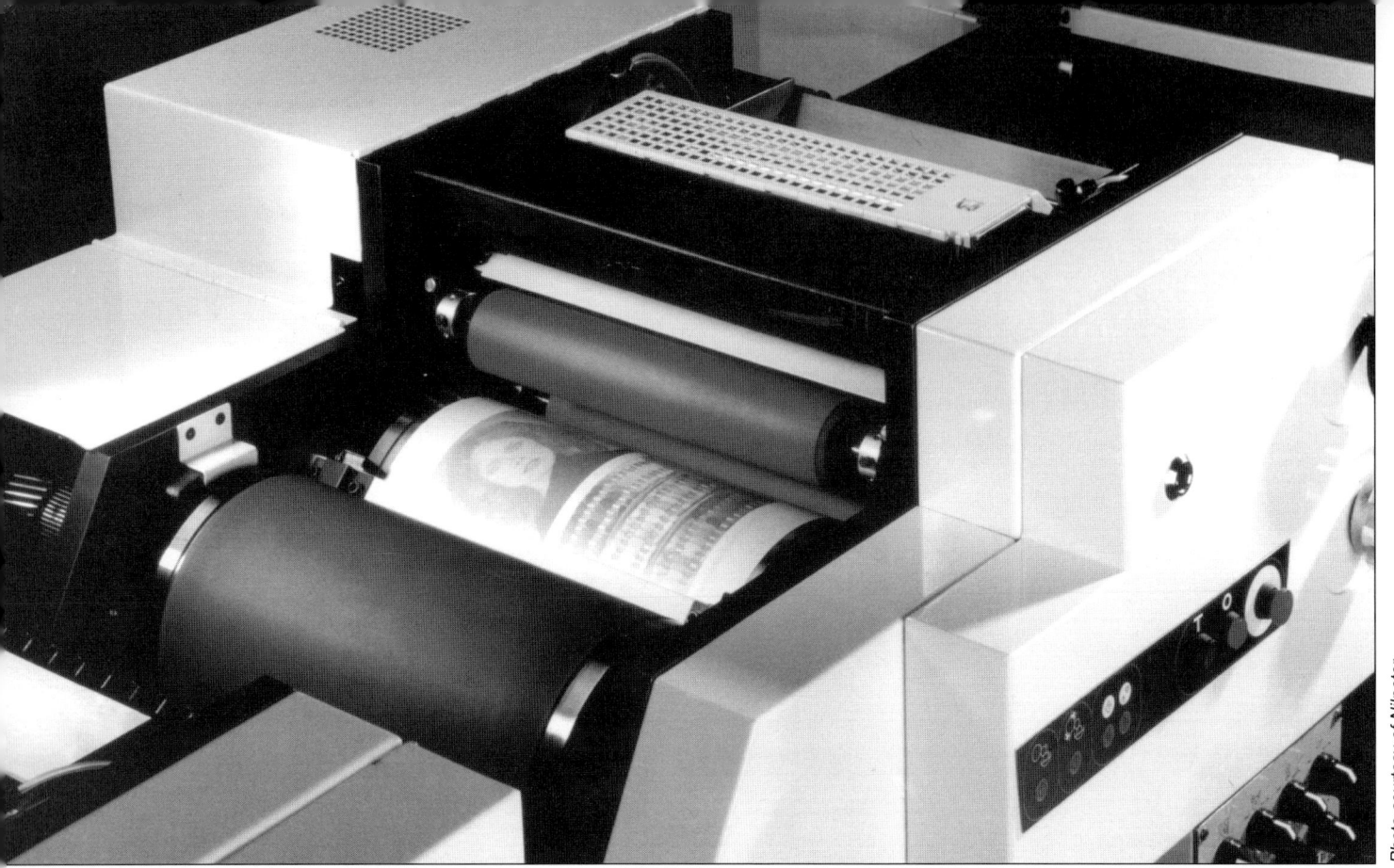

Combination press.

Print Cylinder Setup

Beginning at the front of the supply web, let's look at print cylinder setup. There are an increasing number of tapes that are optimized for combination jobs, and many resources available from leading tape manufacturers to assist with making the proper choice. The main factor, however, is that once you've chosen the correct tape for a given layout, stick with it (no pun intended) so that you remove this variable.

Also, ideally, the plates should be the same – same manufacturer, same type, produced on the same processing equipment. Lastly, proper mounting procedures must be followed – preferably by an experienced, capable mounter, using modern equipment that has been maintained well. There are a variety of high-quality plate-mounting options available today. If you're not using good equipment, then get it ordered, as it will pay for itself very quickly through reduced downtime.

Anilox Rolls

Next, let's look at anilox selection, covering some of the variables that you've probably heard a thousand times. Even though proper anilox selection, use and care should be a given in today's world, it is amazing how often these guidelines are overlooked. A difference in cell volume will affect color density. A plugged or dirty anilox will decrease cell volume.

Ideally, care should be taken to note the anilox ID, not just line count and volume, as different aniloxes will release ink differently. It is also important to use a standard line and volume for different types of work. For instance, using a 500-line/3.2-bcm roll for line work, a 1,000-line/1.2-bcm anilox for process work and a 250-line/5.8-bcm roll for coatings will minimize the typical variation encountered on a daily basis. Additionally, use a regular program of cleaning and monitoring to assure that your aniloxes stay clean.

Inks

Work with your ink supplier to make certain that the inks you're using are designed for the anilox volume you've chosen. There are many ink suppliers available. All offer varying strength levels, and you should not assume that one system will print like another. A difference in strength equals a difference in color density. Also, ink systems can vary in shade, transparency, gloss and viscosity. Water-based inks, for instance, may use different pigments than a UV system, due to the difference in resin chemistry.

When comparing ink systems, ask your supplier for the color index (CI) number, as this is the true identifier of any pigment. Then ask for an ink designed for your anilox volume. You have now made a good start toward comparing "apples to apples." With an eye toward minimizing variables, realize that dot gain, lay, adhesion, gloss and other properties may change with a change in inks.

Substrate Printability

Moving along the supply web, the next topic is substrate. How many shops consider semi-gloss paper to be

Photo courtesy of Nilpeter

their most common stock? Even so, it's amazing how little care is taken in assuring a quality print surface. Is the surface clean and free of dust and contaminants? Do you use a web cleaner, and do you keep the stock storage and pressroom areas clean and free of dust?

A favorite story is about the customer who had a "hickey" problem with the ink. In fact, the regular appearance of these print defects corresponded exactly to the passing of a forklift by the press, which was stirring up a cloud of dust.

These same rules apply if you're running filmic substrates, with the additional variable of dyne level. Care should be taken to check dyne level, with the use of corona treatment or a primer, to alleviate low surface energy. Most ink makers recommend an optimum surface dyne level of 40-46 for best results. With the use of common topcoated stocks, dyne level can become a non-issue, but check for ink/topcoat compatibility before going to press. Some UV inks don't like acrylic topcoats, with adhesion and appearance possibly at risk.

Press Metering System

The metering system on the press must also be considered. The condition and type of doctor blade and/or metering roll material and durometer will greatly affect color density, and therefore overall print quality.

Beveled, rounded, stepped or square – what is the best doctor blade to use? The best bet is to investigate your options, get samples in and set up a test on one print unit with the same anilox and ink, and see which blade gives you the best metering. Armed with these results, an informed decision can be made. Also, train your operators to adjust the metering components with a light touch; minimize pressure whenever possible to prevent premature wear and heat buildup.

Summary

Let's summarize the ways to control variables that can adversely affect quick, profitable job changeovers:
- Print cylinder setup: Standardize mounting tapes for graphic types, narrow plate choices, establish an effective mounting program using modern equipment.

- Aniloxes: Establish standardization program to minimize number, choices; begin and maintain regular cleaning schedule.

- Inks: Choose correct strength level for your jobs, mark shelves clearly, note inks clearly on job ticket.

- Substrate printability: Keep it clean, both in storage and on the press; use corona treatment and web cleaner to control surface dyne level and contamination.

- Press metering system: Regularly examine blade or roller for wear; implement scheduled replacement before wear becomes severe.

How to Save Money

A simple cost justification will convince you that by controlling these variables, you can increase profitability. You can then spend that extra profit on newer technology, which will help speed up your job changes even more. If we examine a theoretical model pressroom, we see:
- 6 presses in the shop;

- 3 jobs per day, per press;

- 1 shift;

- 75 minutes average job changeover time

- $130 per hour in press time

These are fairly conservative values. Most shops run multiple shifts and many more jobs daily. However, this simple model will show us the benefits that can be realized when job changeovers are improved.
- 6 presses X 3 jobs = 18 jobs per day

- 18 jobs/day X 75 minutes = 22.5 hours/day

- Optimization through controlling variables reduces setup by 30 minutes per job, equaling a reduction of 9 hours per day

- 9 hours per day X $130/hour press time X 260 days per year (5 days/week X 52 weeks) = $304,200 MORE PROFIT!

Would this amount help you pay for improved equipment, or another employee that could "float" from press to press, assisting with job setup and changeover? Run this model in your own operation, with your own numbers, and decide for yourself.

Today's quick-change technologies provide many benefits to the printer. Optimization of practices within the pressroom allows total utilization of these technologies by controlling variables that can prevent successful job starts. Documentation of these variables through the use of a job ticket provides a method for achieving this optimized condition, while treating your operation as a series of interrelated links in your internal supply web. Together, these practices add up to a definite advantage for building productivity and increasing profitability.

About the Author...
Ed Dedman is product manager for SICPA North America Inc., and travels North America assisting narrow-web printers with improvements to their operations and overall print quality. He can be reached at ed.dedman@sicpa.com, or at (763) 746-8467.

CONSISTENT COLOR REPRODUCTION

CONTROLLING pH, VISCOSITY IS KEY

By Sean McCardell

As flexographic printing has grown, so has the concern for consistent color reproduction and recognition that a key to this consistency in printing is accurate, precise control of pH and viscosity in flexographic inks. Control will accomplish two very significant benefits for printers: It will cut production costs because ink consumption will be lowered and waste will be reduced; and it will provide consistent color and improve overall print quality.

PH is defined as the degree of alkalinity of an ink. A neutral solution, such as water, measures 7.0 on a scale of 0-14. Higher numbers on the scale indicate an increase in alkalinity—for example, household bleach is extremely alkaline—while lower numbers indicate increased acidity, found in liquids such as vinegar. In terms of water-based flexographic inks, pH levels are typically maintained within a range of 8.6 to 9.2.

Viscosity is defined as an ink's resistance to flow. When we address viscosity in flexographic inks, it is typically measured by comparing the time it takes for a certain amount of ink to empty from a measuring device such as an efflux cup. High viscosity refers to ink that acts thicker, because it travels from the measuring device slower than a low-viscosity ink, which acts thinner.

It is important to note that an ink has one best set point for pH and one best set point for viscosity to achieve optimum color. This is determined by evaluating the condition of all the variables involved in the printing process: press, pumps, anilox roll, printing plates and substrate.

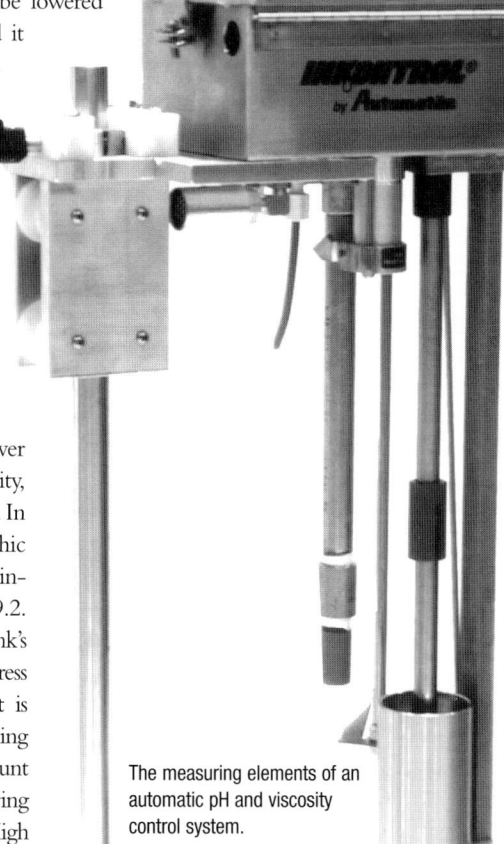

The measuring elements of an automatic pH and viscosity control system.

Ink left sealed in an ink bucket will maintain the same pH level. However, pH levels naturally decrease during a pressrun because amines evaporate from the ink after being exposed to heat and air. This, in turn, lowers the ink pH as it becomes more acidic.

Common factors that influence ink viscosity are the shearing action of pumps and the combination of the shear and heat from the press. These factors result in a reduced, or lower, viscosity. A very important and often overlooked cause of high viscosity is a decrease in the pH level. Because amines are evaporating out of the ink during the pressrun, this causes the resins to fall out, which results in a higher viscosity level.

It is clear that pH and viscosity levels will definitely change throughout a printrun. What are the ramifications when pH and viscosity levels are not corrected? When viscosity levels are too high (meaning the ink flows more slowly), more ink is transferred through the anilox roll and onto the plate, resulting in a stronger color; drying time is slower; more plate wash-ups will be needed, as the tackiness of the ink creates problems on the printing plates; and problems with ink circulation can occur.

When an operator overcorrects for this problem, low viscosity (when the level drops below its appropriate set point and the ink flows more quickly and acts thinner) can occur. Its effects include lighter color than intended; poor coverage; a lack of clear, sharp lines; poor transfer and dry rub resistance; a tendency for ink to dry on the plate; and possible reduction in the ink's shelf life.

In addition to high viscosity, other signs of low pH include an overall muddy appearance because the ink ingredients begin to separate; harder film; difficulty in rewetting the plate; and more difficult clean-up. When

formed in a timely manner instead of waiting until after a change in print quality is noted. Print variations are very gradual, and any change is extremely difficult to notice visually without comparing to a piece printed much earlier. It is imperative that pH and viscosity measurements are performed at least every 15-20 minutes.

Manually measuring pH involves the use of pH

It is important to note
that an ink has one best set point for pH
and one best set point for viscosity to achieve optimum color.
This is determined by evaluating the condition
of all the variables involved in the printing process: press, pumps,
anilox roll, printing plates and substrate.

a pH level rises higher than its desired set point (which can also be caused by an operator's overcorrection), the result can be color burnout, excessive foaming and significant odor problems.

Manual Measuring & Adjusting

Because of the many variations in print quality that can result from incorrect levels, it is extremely important to check levels consistently and to correct them appropriately and in a timely manner. Using inappropriate control methods without determining the real cause for the increased viscosity can result in an erratic cycle of improper levels, with the operator spending valuable time checking the press and other settings and ultimately ending up with inconsistent print results. Therefore, it is crucial to ensure the pH is at the desired set point before adjusting viscosity.

For example, it is very common for the operator—after noticing that the viscosity is increasing—to add water immediately to extend or thin out the ink without first checking the pH. If the increasing viscosity is a result of low pH, the added water does not address the issue of replacing the lost amines that make the ink's pH level correct.

Historically, a trial-and-error approach has been taken in manually controlling pH and viscosity. Usually, even with plant policies and operating procedures in place, checking and adjusting pH and viscosity happens only after a color problem is noted, with manual adjustments usually taking place much later after the fact. It is very important to stress to press operators that the measurements should be per-

probes. After the operator has successfully printed the first acceptable sheet, the pH must be read and recorded for future use. Periodically, the operator must take a reading to ensure that it is kept within range. This is accomplished by inserting a pH probe into the ink and waiting for a reading. If the pH reading comes back with a low reading, the operator puts in a correcting solution. This process is repeated until the pH is back in range.

Manually measuring viscosity requires use of a measuring device, such as an efflux cup, and a stopwatch. The process involves many steps, which must be followed carefully:

1. Take measurements in a room free of drafts and dramatic changes in temperature (room temperature should be between 76-78 degrees F.).

2. Cap the measuring cup and hold it upright.

3. Fill the cup with ink. Ensure that there are no lumps of foam or other contaminants; these will make an accurate reading impossible. At the same time, remove the cap to allow the liquid to drain and start the stopwatch. The cup must be level.

4. Time (in seconds) the drainage of the ink from the cup to the moment when the first break in the stream occurs (called the stop point).

A significant problem with manual measurements is that no two people will get the same result. The time of starting and stopping the watch will be different for each person. This is important because published reports indicate that a slight deviation in viscosity can mean a significant difference in ink mileage, density and drying rate, equating to an excess ink laydown.

Manual control of pH and viscosity is possible, but is often considered an unpopular task in the plant, and—as you can see—has significant potential to be inaccurate.

Automated Systems

An automatic pH and viscosity control system is necessary to achieve constant and uniform ink color and laydown. In today's cost-conscious production environments, it becomes apparent that the practice of manual measurement and adjustment is no longer adequate to achieve consistent color reproduction. Automated systems truly make new levels of quality and efficiency a reality.

For viscosity control in an automated system, a piston and cylinder are utilized. The operator enters into the computer a desired viscosity setting. The piston is periodically raised to the top of the cylinder, drawing ink into the cylinder through an orifice at the bottom. The piston is then released and allowed to fall by the force of gravity, expelling the ink through the same path that it entered. The time of fall measurement is sent to the processor and recorded in seconds.

When a proximity sensor detects that the viscosity exceeds the desired setting, a valve is opened that dispenses a let-down solution in small quantities into the ink. This process is repeated until the viscosity returns to the desired set point.

After a correction has been made, the unit will continue to monitor viscosity and display the value. The system is designed to prevent overcorrection by allowing the solution to completely mix the ink. This is accomplished with a continuous gentle stirring action by the agitator.

For pH control, the operator also enters the desired pH setting into the computer program, usually stepping the pH from high to low between colors. The pH sensor, mounted onto the measuring unit, is lowered into the ink bucket, where it comes in contact with the ink and begins reading hydrogen ion activity. The pH sensor reports this information to the computer, which then compares that value with the desired setting. If the pH is lower than the set point, a valve is energized that disperses small quantities of correction solution. This process is repeated until the pH level returns to its set point.

An additional feature of automated control systems is the capability to monitor and display temperature for reference. This reading is continuously displayed, which will assist the operator in easily identifying extreme temperature changes in the ink.

Test Compares Manual, Automatic

To substantiate the effects of an automated system vs. manual methods of controlling pH and viscosity, a test was performed on a flexo printing press comparing the two methods. An automated control system was used for two pressruns that were conducted with all conditions and variables held constant. For the first run, the automated system was put into manual mode, in which all measurements and adjustments were done by the press operators. During the second pressrun, the system was put into automatic mode, with measurements and adjustments being made by the system. The results of both runs were recorded, charted and compared.

With manual measurements, operator checks of pH and viscosity occurred most often after the fact (i.e., when a printing variation was noted), and aggressive adjustments triggered another set of undesirable conditions. More time was then spent chasing pH and viscosity than attending to other aspects of the print job. Remember that a slight deviation in viscosity can result in a significant increase in ink laydown.

In automatic mode, pH and viscosity measurements and adjustments were made by the system and not the operator. Viscosity was consistently maintained. The erratic variations that occurred during manual mode were resolved with automatic control. Deviations from the set point were negligent. The system automatically checked pH and viscosity in a more timely and consistent manner and ruled out human error. To achieve this manually would require a significant investment in a technician's time and effort. Even then, it would be difficult to accomplish consistency in the readings.

Automatic Benefits

The benefits of automatic control are tremendous:
- Consistent color gain. Hickeys, inconsistent ink density and muddying print characteristics due to improper viscosity or pH levels are eliminated.

- Reduction of ink consumption. PH and viscosity levels relate directly to the characteristics of flexo inks, affecting the anilox-plate and plate-substrate ink transfer. Users report using up to one fewer kit of ink per run period because less ink is wasted when pH and viscosity are constant. You will no longer be adjusting with fresh ink, but rather with a prescribed let-down solution.

- Cost decrease. The entire flexo printing operation runs more efficiently and cost-effectively with auto matic flexo ink pH and viscosity control. Color consistency is more a function of maintaining the delicate balance in the ink properties during the run than of the price paid for the ink.

- Elimination of plate washup by as much as 95 percent. Incorrect levels of pH and viscosity result in more frequent need for printing plate washups.

- Significant ink foaming reduction. Anti-foam additives are more effective because of the built-in circulation feature in automatic systems.

- Increased management quality. Human error and effort in manually measuring pH and viscosity is eliminated. An automated system is very precise and requires little crew time and attention.

- Simplification of the documentation process. Gathering and storing job information is made simple, which is helpful for in-house record keeping and ISO 9000 documentation purposes.

- Improvement of product quality and productivity. Most importantly are the benefits of improved product quality and productivity when using an automated system.

Gaining control of pH and viscosity, two very sensitive and critical variables, is the key to achieving consistent color reproduction in printing, reducing waste and lowering ink consumption.

About the Author...
Sean McCardell is with Automatän Inc., manufacturer of Inkontrol® automatic pH and viscosity control systems and based in Plover, WI.

BENCHMARK TESTING

KEY TO SUCCESS FOR LABELS AND MORE

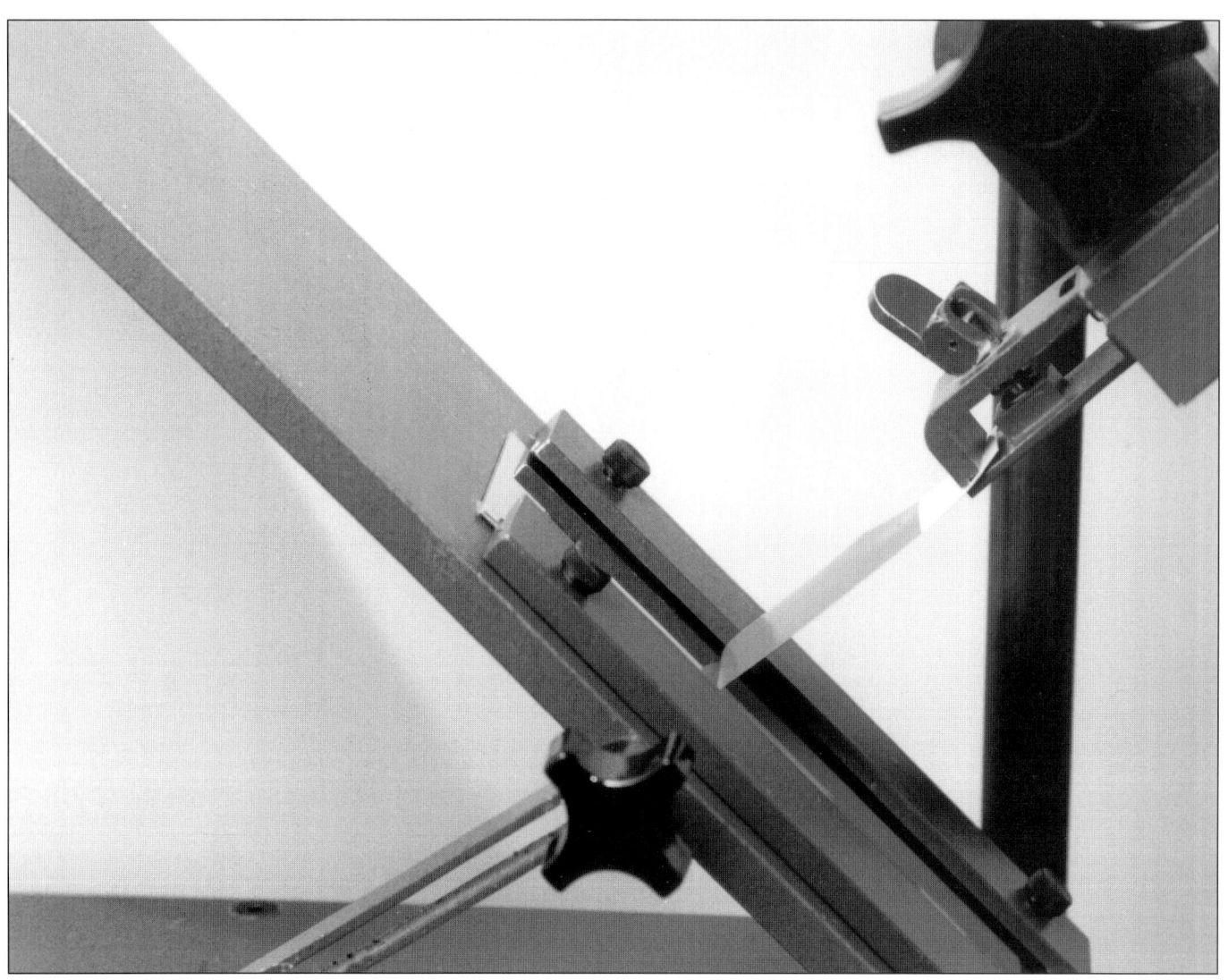

Peel adhesion is the measure of force required to remove an adhesive from a substrate material under a standard set of conditions.

By Donald L. Eppink

Did you ever wonder how successful companies stay successful? The answer is focus! Successful companies focus on what they are good at, on improving or eliminating the bad, and using the good to plan for the future. And how do they focus? One way is through benchmark testing.

What is benchmark testing? It is a reference point; a set of objective results for comparing your current products and judging your future products or services. It is not difficult to do and it doesn't have to be expensive. It is a way to understand the properties of your products and those of your competitors, an important means toward gaining a competitive edge in the marketplace.

You can design a benchmark program and get payback. The more thorough the program, the bigger the payback. The testing part is simple. It is a tool for learning from your products and experiences and those of others in your field. It is a tool that provides insight into the strengths and weaknesses of your current technology; a baseline for future decisions and growth. Four reasons to benchmark test are: knowledge, quality, development strategies and marketing options. This article will explain these advantages and their key features in more detail.

Reasons to Benchmark

Product Knowledge. You can't build a house without a foundation! The same applies to products; you can't build products without a baseline! Have you ever tried to fix something without knowing what was wrong? Have you ever given a sales pitch to a customer about your product only to find that it really didn't work that well?

Many of us perceive benchmark testing as something only suppliers do. But we are all suppliers of goods or services in some form. We purchase from our vendors, add value, then sell to our customers. It is to our advantage to have as much knowledge as possible about our products and those of our competitors, whether we're buying or selling.

Product Quality. When representative product samples are benchmark tested, the results may be accu-

rate, but they are from only one snapshot in time. It may be desirable to perform the testing periodically throughout the year. We are all aware that many processes display seasonal variations. Periodic testing allows you to document the extent of the variability or assure the products are not significantly changing. This historical database can prove invaluable should a customer question the product performance of shipments from a particular time period. Periodic testing can also allow observation of your competitors' reproducibility.

Purchase Specifications. Benchmark testing provides a database that allows you to establish purchase specifications that meet the requirements of your process

or product. Vendors often supply you with data sheets outlining their products' typical values. Most of the time these products work well, but occasionally they may not. The reason may be that the product's variability is greater than your process will tolerate. By benchmarking incoming products from various suppliers over a period of time, a set of specifications can be established that, when met, assures incoming materials yield consistent results. Benchmarking your products also provides a valuable database when customers ask your assistance in establishing their purchase specifications.

Product Development. Another reason to perform benchmark testing lies in the critical area of product development. As product suppliers in a dynamic marketplace, we need to know how our products compare to our competitors'. Using an objective set of standards and testing without bias, much can be learned

A shear test measures the internal strength, or guts, of the adhesive.

about how your products stack up in the marketplace. This is true whether it is a consumer commodity or in a specialized niche industry. By going nose-to-nose with your competitors' products objectively, you can obtain a good understanding of each product's strengths and weaknesses. This knowledge can then serve as an excellent platform for future product development.

Marketing Strategies. Marketing strategies can be built around the results of benchmark testing. A completed protocol of objective standards can allow you to make subjective or relative statements. You may now state with confidence that your product has twice the holding power as the leading brand or a more stable viscosity over a range of temperatures. You have the facts to prove it! A thorough knowledge of benchmark data and its relevancy allows you to weed out accurate but misleading claims.

Over the last few years, we have seen a rise in the number of requests for third-party, objective, competitive benchmark testing. In each case, the results have always been eye opening for the client. In some cases, the benchmark study confirmed their current speculation based on field feedback. In other cases, it stopped the introduction of products before they became an embarrassment to the company.

Qualities of Benchmark Testing

In order to be accurate and significant, benchmark testing must possess at least four qualities.

1. Testing must be objective and quantifiable. To be objective is to be real. Successful companies have learned to be objective with their benchmark testing. This "honesty" in testing allows them to see clearly and plan for the future based on the knowledge they have gained.

The properties tested must be quantifiable in a reproducible manner. Benchmarking is not a set of subjective impressions of how a product feels, looks or smells. Quantification demands that precision instrumentation be utilized that is accurately calibrated and recognized as suitable for the test. The reproducibility of the test methods must extend over time and with a diversity of operators.

2. The properties being tested must be significant. Each test performed must be relevant to characterize some real-world property of the product. If color or tensile strength or adhesion over time is important for the product, test it. If it's not, don't.

3. The product being tested must be representative of its group. If production material is the subject of the test, it must be a properly documented random sample. That is, its manufacturing control (date, lot number, etc.) is to be noted, but it should not be selected because it ran better than the product has for a long time. If it is a developmental product, it must represent material that at least can be reproduced.

4. All products should have similar histories. It would be unfair to compare a freshly manufactured product against one that has been in storage under unknown conditions for an extended period of time. This also applies when competitors' products are tested. If benchmarking competitive products, it is a good idea to purchase all samples from either retail or wholesale sources rather than pulling your own out of inventory.

Typical Benchmark Protocol

Benchmarking a group of products requires that measured characteristics be significant and relevant to real-world properties. For example, suppose you, as a pressure-sensitive label manufacturer, want to compare the products of your present supplier to those of several other vendors.

What would you do to assure you are using the best, or perhaps the most cost effective stock? What characteristics should be tested to allow you to make a knowledgeable decision with confidence?

Our experience suggests that you need to test at least the following five characteristics:

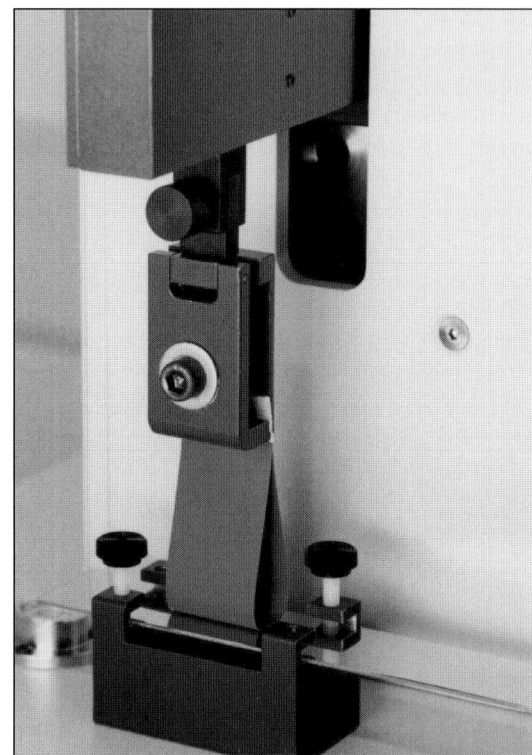

The loop tack method of measuring PSA grip can be used successfully over a wide range of adhesive types.

• Peel Adhesion

• Tack

• Cohesion (shear resistance)

• Release

• Coat weight

You may need to test these characteristics when the labels are applied on different substrates, depending on the end use of the product. You may also need to see how the characteristics change upon aging, either prior to application (as might be experienced sitting in a warehouse) or after application (how well it holds up in use).

Peel Adhesion (ASTM D 3330, PSTC-101) is a measure of the force required to remove an adhesive from a substrate material under a standard set of conditions. There are many variables in the process (application pressure and time, substrate surface finish, temperature, dwell time between application and removal, removal speed, removal angle and so forth), all of which need to be precisely controlled to achieve comparative results. It is important during testing to note not only the magnitude of the force measured, but the mode of failure as well. Does the adhesive leave a residue or a shadow on the substrate? Does the adhesive split? Is the peel smooth or zippery?

Tack is a measure of the instantaneous grip of a PSA. A number of techniques are used in the industry to measure this characteristic: by probe, rolling ball, or loop (ASTM D 2979, PSTC-16, TLMI Loop Tack). We prefer to use loop tack because this method can be used successfully over a wide range of adhesive types, it tests a larger sample surface area and is the best for distinguishing modes of failure.

Shear is a measure of the internal strength, or guts, of the adhesive. A known surface area of the label material is applied to a standard surface. The substrate is held at an angle of 1 degree from vertical and a weight is applied to the end of the label (ASTM D 6463, PSTC-107, TLMI Static Shear). The shear is measured as the amount of time required for the sample to fall off the substrate. As with the peel adhesion test, a number of test parameters must be kept constant.

Release is the amount of force required to remove the liner from the label stock (ASTM D 5375, PSTC-4B, TLMI Liner Release). It is best to test this characteristic at, or at least near, typical application speed. Parameters need to be constant when testing each material. A precision instrument is required to achieve accurate results.

Coat Weight is a measure of the amount of adhesive on the label, measured either by thickness or in amount per unit area (ASTM D 3652, PSTC-33, TLMI Coat Weight). Thickness can be measured with an anvil micrometer, although accuracy may be sacrificed if the stock is not of uniform caliper. In many cases a more accurate method for determining coat weight is by the solvent wash-off method. A sample of known area is usually die cut to a standard dimension. The liner is removed and the sample is accurately weighed. The adhesive is then removed using one of a variety of organic solvents, dried, then reweighed. By calculating the weight difference, the coat weight can easily be calculated.

The standard test methods referenced above are not exclusive; they are simply the most common. As the marketplace becomes more global, there is a move to find common ground among professional societies and establish methods accepted universally.

Other specialized tests are also important when characterizing products that have been developed for a specific end-use. Mandrel holding power; testing at high or low temperatures; testing after accelerated aging in heat, humid and UV environments; and SAFT (Shear Adhesion Failure Temperature) testing are just a few of the special end use-tests that should be included in benchmark testing some products.

It goes without saying that all testing must be performed a number of times on a given sample to have assurances that the data produced is reasonably accurate and precise. Typically, most of these tests are conducted with a minimum of five replicates per sample, sometimes more, occasionally less.

Testing Facilities

Testing of this nature requires precision instrumentation: an adhesion/release tester, a shear tester, timers, tack tester, roll-down equipment, sample cutters, analytical balance, precision dies, an oven and micrometers, among others, and a room with a controlled environment to house them. It is critical that the equipment and environmental conditions specified in the test methods are used for each test. This assures a minimization of the measurement uncertainty. Through round-robin testing we've learned that improperly maintained or calibrated equipment and an uncontrolled environment can adversely affect data.

Decisions based on the results of a benchmark study are only as good as the data. The knowledge that all testing was performed according to standard methods on suitable, accurate equipment allows decisions to be made with confidence.

The benchmark testing you need to compete and grow can be performed at a competitive price through an independent testing facility. By contracting with an independent laboratory, recognized in its field of specialization, you can be assured of impartial results. If that laboratory is also nationally accredited, you are confident the results are accurate because the lab's competency has been reviewed by a recognized third party. You can also count on its expertise to help you interpret the results.

Why You Need Benchmark Testing

With the results of a benchmark study in hand, you have greater knowledge of your product and its place in the market. You know where you stand in relation to your competition. It ensures that a quality product is being manufactured or opens opportunities for improvement. You have facts from which purchase specifications can be established and development strategies finalized. The results can be marketed to your advantage.

Benchmark testing is a means to determine the reality of the moment and provide the basis for future efforts. Successful companies stay successful by being focused. Benchmark testing is one of the keys they use to maintain that focus. If you've been planning on doing a benchmark study but have been waiting for the right moment, the time has never been better.

About the Author...
Donald L. Eppink (deppink@chemsultants.com) is manager of laboratory services at Chemsultants Inc., an A2LA-accredited, independent laboratory specializing in the compounding, coating and testing of adhesives products. He has over 30 years of R&D, process/product engineering, quality and laboratory testing experience.

Cutting Corrugated Waste
How to Make Your Plant More Profitable

By Brent Daisley

In general, waste is the biggest single area where profits are torn up and lost. Waste figures for the world's best corrugating plants are in the order of about 5 percent. This figure should be the aim for all box plants. The best definition of waste is: any piece of paper or board that is not sold for the exact purpose for which it was bought. Thus, even tie sheets, protectors, dunnage and slip-sheets should all be counted as waste.

The place where most waste is actually generated is on the corrugator—the largest single area in a box plant one can investigate to save money. Often, if management and technical staff make the operations better on the corrugator, savings are automatically generated in downstream equipment such as presses and die cutters. One way to reduce waste at the printing and converting area is to use flat, well-made board. Producing flat board contributes the following major benefits to a corrugated converter:

• Waste, based on area, is usually halved in the converting area.

• Converting machine speeds increase by 27 percent.

• Corrugator running speeds increase by 21 percent.

• Overall productivity increases by 32 percent.

(Based on a study by TAPPI (Technical Asssociation of the Pulp and Paper Industry.)

Let's take a look at how you can investigate each piece of equipment downstream from the corrugator to eliminate waste and save money. Every equipment change you make to cut waste adds profit to the bottom line of a box plant; when combined, these changes allow massive increases in profit.

Core Chucks, Reel Stands

The point where your paper initially meets your corrugator is the core chucks (and reel stands). The correct core chuck will have the ability to manage different size cores; be easy to use; require little or no maintenance; and can use all the paper that is on

> **T**he place where most waste
> is actually generated
> is on the corrugator—
> the largest single area
> in a box plant one can investigate
> to save money.

the core. The core chuck should not damage the paper core, preventing core re-use by the paper company.

A chuck must automatically align the paper roll on the centerline of the corrugator. Edge misalignment is a major cause of waste. A chuck that possesses the above characteristics will instantly save you money by allowing all your expensive paper to be used, while perhaps also allowing a small monetary refund from your paper supplier by allowing it to re-use cores. A chuck that does not have the above characteristics will lose money. Good chucks have a typical ROI (return on investment) of around three to six months.

Cross Machine Web Tension

Your standard adjustable wrap arm rolls (just before each preheater) should be examined and, if worn out, replaced. Often, worn out, non-self-align-

A good corrugating roll can save a plant tens of thousands of dollars per year. These rolls should be super-precise, with the absolute latest technology in respect to roll coatings.

ing components lead to massive paper wastage downstream of their location by causing wrinkling and bagging through uneven heat transfer. These standard items cause loose or tight edges in the paper over the preheaters, which in turn causes uneven moisture removal, thus creating warp. A tight edge removes more moisture than a loose edge. Less moisture (a loose edge) on the double-facer liner drive side will cause down-warp on the drive side and up-warp on the operator side. More moisture on the double facer operator side causes the reverse condition.

A good cross-machine web-tensioning device should "react" to the web rather than try to "steer" it. If a system attempts to steer the web, it can cause the web to become misaligned, greatly increasing waste. The equipment should be 100 percent mechanical rather than pneumatic or electrical in nature. It should be easy to install and have very low maintenance requirements.

The most important feature that the web tensioning system must have is a 360-degree correction capability. Otherwise, it will not work as efficiently and will limit its location(s). A good system will eliminate cross-web tension problems; improve board quality; reduce warp and delamination; and increase corrugator running speeds. Typical ROI of a good cross-machine web tensioning system is three to six months.

Such rolls must be placed as close to the preheater as possible; these rolls should be the entry rolls to the preheater, whether fixed or adjustable. If they are placed more than 500 millimeters away from the preheater, they may cause edge misalignment.

Corrugating Rolls

You have probably heard the saying that corrugating rolls are the heart of a corrugator, with board quality being set at the corrugating rolls. The most important characteristics of a good corrugating roll are:

• Flute profile.

• Tension build-up in the labyrinth, caused by the friction of the paper sliding over the flutes.

• Thermal stability. Uniform and constant surface tem-

peratures are necessary for good flute formation.

• Correct crown.

• Absolute precision, measured in a few microns.

A good corrugating roll can save a plant tens of thousands—and even hundreds of thousands—of dollars per year, depending on total tonnage of the plant. Savings are generated through using less substrate, without sacrificing box strength. These rolls should be super-precise, with the absolute latest technology in respect to roll coatings. They should have better runability on all grades of paper, should last much longer than inferior rolls and should result in better, stronger board for the life of the roll.

The rolls should also allow faster running speeds due to decreased paper tension in the labyrinth between the rolls, which results in less corrugator vibration and noise. It is important that the rolls be able to run at full speed immediately after installation (no running in) and have minimal, if any, bow (banana effect) after single-facer stoppages. Rolls should have optimized flute profiles, allowing less substrate to be used, which saves large amounts of money on paper purchases. The enjoyed savings in paper usage, coupled with the above characteristics, means a typical ROI on such rolls would be achieved in about three to 12 months, depending on paper usage.

Neglecting to purchase a good corrugating roll will cost a plant a great deal of money that could have otherwise been saved. All modern corrugating rolls today are plasma spray-coated with super-hard Tungsten Carbide in a Cobalt metal matrix base which increases roll life two to five times over chromed rolls. Chromed corrugating rolls are now obsolete, old technology.

Rider Rolls

The next item downstream one should examine is the liner moisture and adhesive application at the point where the single-face and double-face sides of the corrugated board come together – your rider rolls. (The rider roll is the chromed idler roll above the starch applicator roll.) Standard rider rolls should be replaced with a spring-loaded bar with polished stainless steel shoes that automatically adjusts up and down for various grades of board being passed through it. That is just not possible on standard rider roll machines. Such a bar allows even pressure on the single-face web onto the glue roll, no matter what medium or liner or flute height is introduced. Even gentle pressure allows the flutes to come into contact with the glue roll without crushing them while also reducing adhesive consumption.

By avoiding crush at this stage, some plants have been able to substitute lighter grades of paper while achieving the same box strength. This saves massive amounts on paper purchases, typically between 2 percent and 4 percent. Such a bar with spring loaded stainless steel shoes will also help you achieve greater consistency, reduced variability, increased predictability and increased confidence when it comes to making flat, strong board.

The Double Backer

Downstream of this is where the actual bonding of the single-face web and the double-face liner occurs: the double backer heating section. The combined board created in this section will affect the quality of the sheets and boxes that are produced downstream. For that reason, this is another important area on the corrugator to look at waste reduction. Most warp is caused in the heating section by varying heat; and by excess heat applied to the board, or heat applied too fast.

Typical of this section are the steam chests and weight or ballast rolls. As the board passes over this section, it causes a heat differential between the bottom and the top of the steam chests, resulting in the chests warping or sagging. This causes two problems for the board as the chests sag: delamination of the board that is not coming into contact with the chest in the middle section; and edge crush, as the weight and ballast rolls tend to crush the board at their outer edges due to increased weight (support) in this area. When the hotplates bend down, all the weight of the rolls is concentrated on just the edges of the board, creating edge crush.

To overcome this, a plant needs spring-loaded devices that can contour to the sag of the chests, especially as temperature differential increases (causing greater sag). The replacement of the weight/ballast rolls with a series of spring-loaded stainless steel shoes greatly increases even heat transfer both across and along the board. With such a system, a plant can greatly reduce warp of any description—as well as edge crush and delamination—which eliminates a great

deal of waste. Each bar should be raised and lowered, semi- or fully automatically, under a PLC control to keep the heat constant.

All modern double backers are roll-less; i.e., there are no weight rolls at all in either the heating section or cooling/traction section.

Warp Costs Money

Warp is a major problem for box plant owners. Its associated problems of corrugator overtime due to slower running speeds and its greater consumption of paper, starch/gas and electricity all greatly reduce the profits of a box plant. Add to that all the associated problems downstream of the corrugator, such as soft sheets that won't die cut cleanly; "washboard" sheets that won't print properly without crushing; and the dramatic increase of waste due to reduced printing and slotting register.

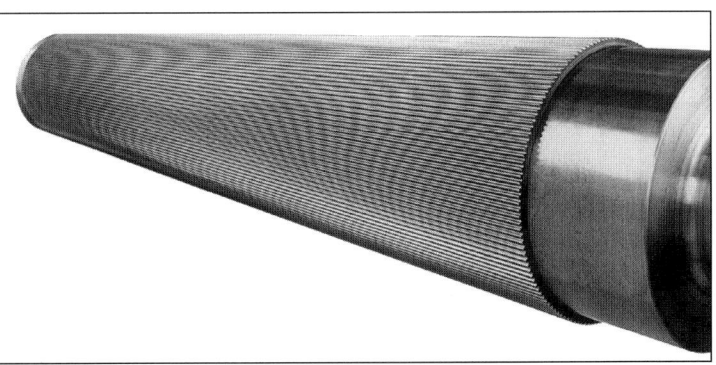

Speed Synchronization

Several other factors can greatly increase a box plant's profits. One is whether the single facer is run in speed synchronization with the double facer. A simple speed-control/synchronizing device is necessary to combat the effects of warp. Corrugators operated in unsynchronized (manual) mode generate large amounts of "normal" and "reverse" warp. The bridge control, as it is called, must make the single facer run so as to keep the bridge almost empty and constant.

If you are not employing the above practices in your corrugator plant, you are simply losing money you do not necessarily have to lose. By following these simple processes and adopting the right techniques and the right equipment, you can make your box plant operations more profitable. 🔲

About the Author...
Brent Daisley is customer service manager for Brently Engineering Pty. Ltd., Sydney, Australia. Brently sources, supplies and services the corrugated and converting industry in the Asia-Pacific region. For more information, contact Brently Engineering at 61-2-94271177 (phone), 61-2-94270477 (fax) or brently@brently.com (email); or log on to the company's web site at www.brently.com.